D1203273

The Blackbirch Visual Encyclopedia

Places of the World

BLACKBIRCH®
PRESS

THOMSON

GALE

San Diego • Detroit • New York • San Francisco • Cleveland • New Haven, Conn. • Waterville, Maine • London • Munich

CONTENTS

THOMSON

GALE

© 2002 by Blackbirch Press™. Blackbirch Press™ is an imprint of The Gale Group, Inc., a division of Thomson Learning, Inc.

Blackbirch Press™ and Thomson Learning™ are trademarks used herein under license.

For more information, contact
The Gale Group, Inc.
27500 Drake Rd.
Farmington Hills, MI 48331-3535
Or you can visit our Internet site at http://www.gale.com

Copyright © 2000 Orpheus Books Ltd. Created and produced by Nicholas Harris, Joanna Turner, and Claire Aston, Orpheus Books Ltd.

Every effort has been made to trace the owners of copyrighted material.

Text credit: Claire Aston

Illustration credit: Gary Hincks, Steve Noon

Map on pages 4-5: Olive Pearson

LIBRARY OF CONGRESS CATALOGING-IN-PUBLICATION DATA

Harris, Nicholas, 1956-
Places of the world / Nicholas Harris.
      p. cm. — (Blackbirch visual encyclopedia)
   Includes index.
   Summary: A visual encyclopedia of six continents plus Oceania, highlighting significant facts and features of each region.
   ISBN 1-56711-517-9 (lib. bdg. : alk. paper)
   1. Children's atlases. 2. Geography. [1. Atlases. 2. Geography—Encyclopedias.] I. Blackbirch Press. II. Title. III. Series.
G1021 .H59847 2002
912—dc21   2002031016

Printed in Singapore
10 9 8 7 6 5 4 3 2 1

CONTENTS

THE WORLD

North America
South America
Europe
Africa
Asia
Oceania

A.	Andorra	CO.	Côte d'Ivoire
AL.	Albania	CR.	Croatia
AR.	Armenia	CZ.	Czech Republic
AZ.	Azerbaijan	E.G.	Equatorial Guinea
AU.	Austria	ES.	Estonia
B.	Bahrain	FR.	France
BE.	Belgium	GE.	Georgia
BO.	Bosnia-Herzegovina	GH.	Ghana
BU.	Burundi	GR.	Grenada

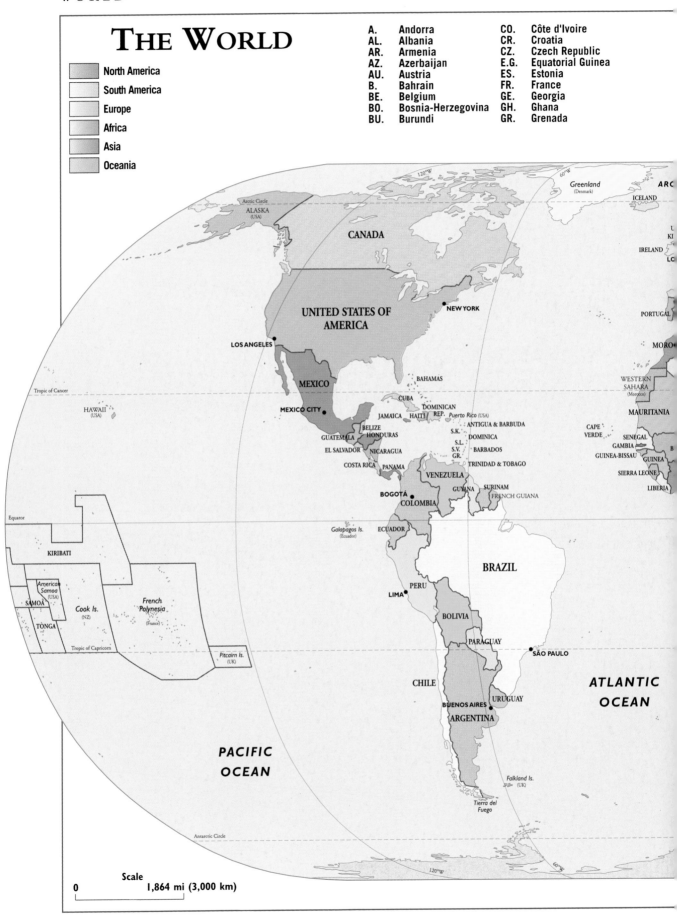

ARC

Greenland
(Denmark)

ICELAND

Arctic Circle

ALASKA
(USA)

CANADA

IRELAND

KI

LO

UNITED STATES OF
AMERICA

NEW YORK

PORTUGAL

LOS ANGELES

MORO

BAHAMAS

WESTERN
SAHARA
(Morocco)

MEXICO

CUBA

Tropic of Cancer

HAWAII
(USA)

MEXICO CITY

DOMINICAN
REP. Puerto Rico (USA)

JAMAICA HAITI

MAURITANIA

ANTIGUA & BARBUDA

BELIZE
HONDURAS

S.K.

DOMINICA

CAPE
VERDE

SENEGAL

GUATEMALA

EL SALVADOR NICARAGUA

S.L.
S.V.
GR.

BARBADOS

GAMBIA

GUINEA-BISSAU

GUINEA

B

COSTA RICA PANAMA

TRINIDAD & TOBAGO

SIERRA LEONE

VENEZUELA

LIBERIA

BOGOTÁ

GUYANA SURINAM
FRENCH GUIANA

COLOMBIA

Equator

KIRIBATI

Galapagos Is.
(Ecuador)

ECUADOR

BRAZIL

American
Samoa
(USA)

SAMOA

Cook Is.
(NZ)

French
Polynesia
(France)

PERU

LIMA

BOLIVIA

TONGA

PARAGUAY

SÃO PAULO

Tropic of Capricorn

Pitcairn Is.
(UK)

ATLANTIC
OCEAN

CHILE

URUGUAY

BUENOS AIRES

PACIFIC
OCEAN

ARGENTINA

Falkland Is.
(UK)

Tierra del
Fuego

Antarctic Circle

Scale

0   1,864 mi (3,000 km)

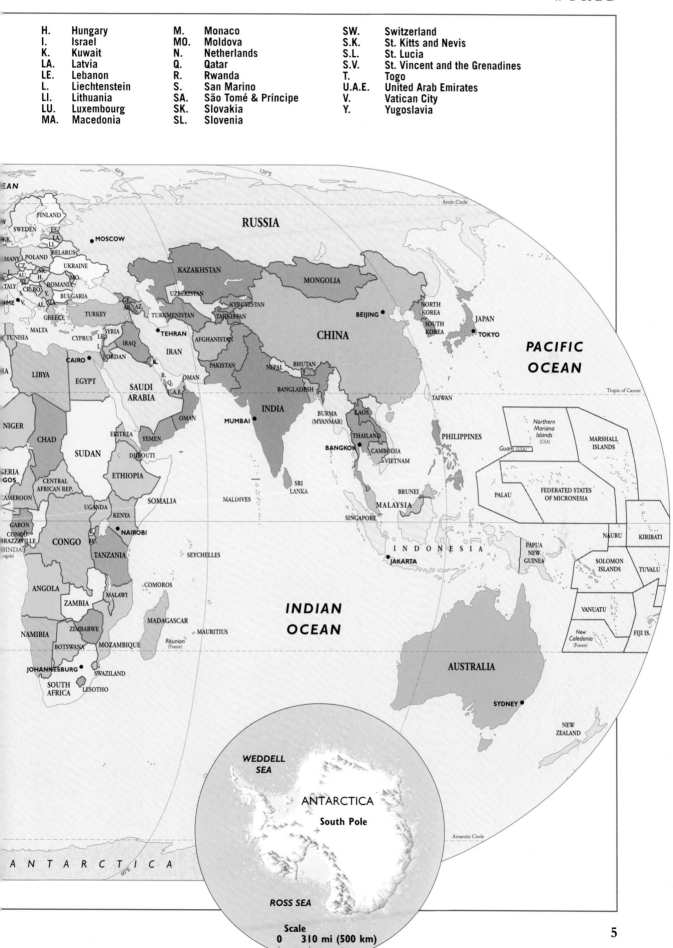

H.	Hungary	M.	Monaco	SW.	Switzerland
I.	Israel	MO.	Moldova	S.K.	St. Kitts and Nevis
K.	Kuwait	N.	Netherlands	S.L.	St. Lucia
LA.	Latvia	Q.	Qatar	S.V.	St. Vincent and the Grenadines
LE.	Lebanon	R.	Rwanda	T.	Togo
L.	Liechtenstein	S.	San Marino	U.A.E.	United Arab Emirates
LI.	Lithuania	SA.	São Tomé & Príncipe	V.	Vatican City
LU.	Luxembourg	SK.	Slovakia	Y.	Yugoslavia
MA.	Macedonia	SL.	Slovenia		

Scale
0   310 mi (500 km)

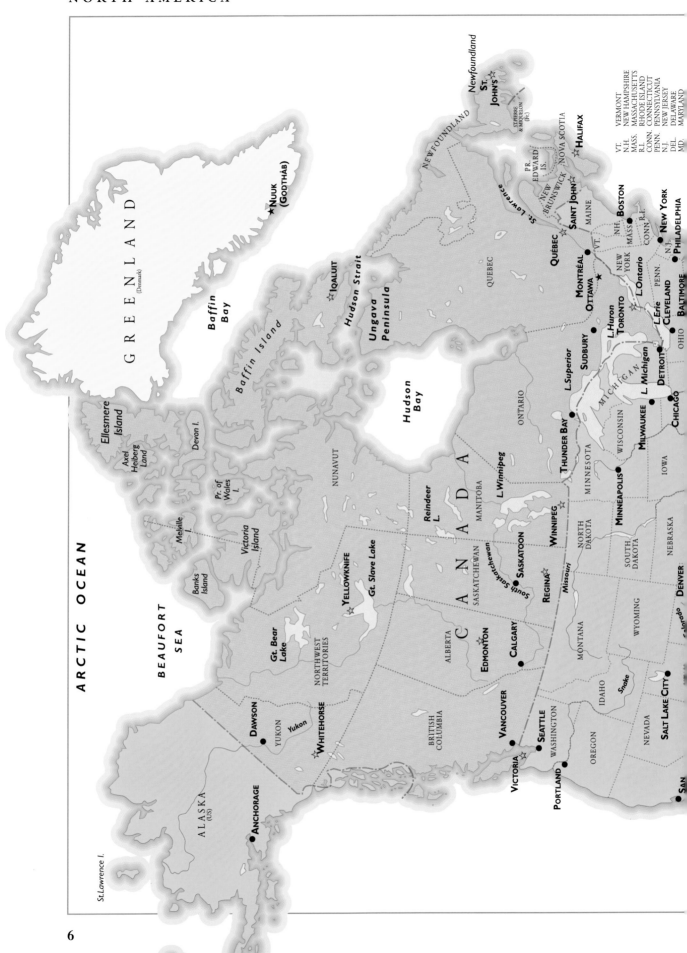

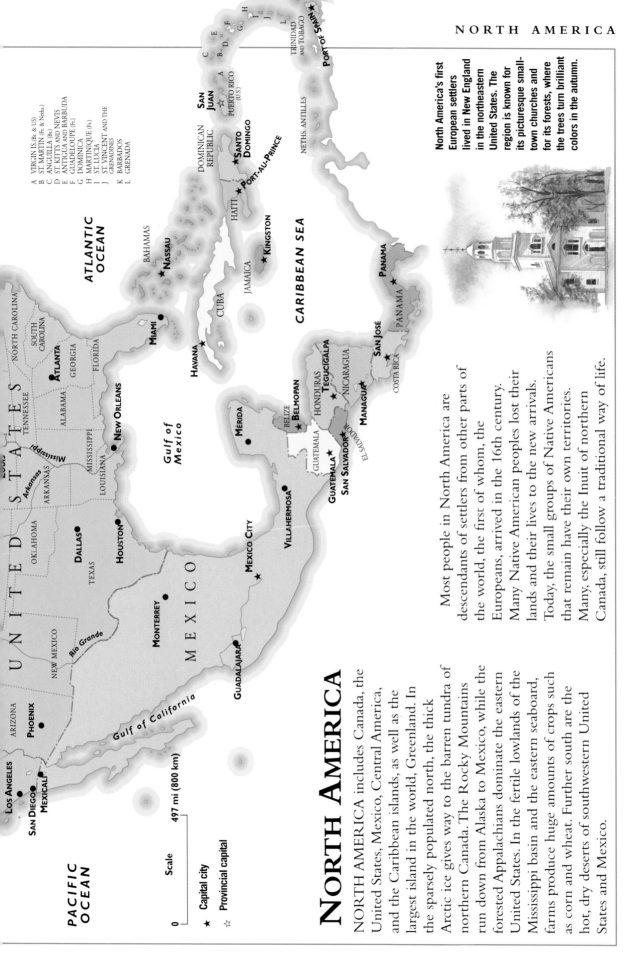

PACIFIC
OCEAN

Scale

0   497 mi (800 km)

★ Capital city

☆ Provincial capital

ATLANTIC
OCEAN

A VIRGIN IS.(Br. & US)
B ST. MARTIN (Fr. & Neths.)
C ANGUILLA (Br.)
D ST. KITTS AND NEVIS
E ANTIGUA AND BARBUDA
F GUADELOUPE (Fr.)
G DOMINICA
H MARTINIQUE (Fr.)
I ST. LUCIA
J ST. VINCENT AND THE
   GRENADINES
K BARBADOS
L GRENADA

CARIBBEAN SEA

PORT OF SPAIN

TRINIDAD AND TOBAGO

NETHS. ANTILLES

SAN JUAN
PUERTO RICO (U.S.)

SANTO DOMINGO
DOMINICAN REPUBLIC

PORT-AU-PRINCE
HAITI

KINGSTON
JAMAICA

CUBA
HAVANA

NASSAU
BAHAMAS

MIAMI

ATLANTA
GEORGIA
FLORIDA

NORTH CAROLINA
SOUTH CAROLINA
TENNESSEE
ALABAMA

UNITED STATES

NEW ORLEANS
MISSISSIPPI
LOUISIANA
ARKANSAS
Arkansas
Mississippi

Gulf of
Mexico

PANAMA
PANAMA

SAN JOSÉ
COSTA RICA

MANAGUA
NICARAGUA

TEGUCIGALPA
HONDURAS

BELMOPAN
BELIZE

SAN SALVADOR
EL SALVADOR

GUATEMALA
GUATEMALA

MÉRIDA

VILLAHERMOSA

MEXICO CITY

DALLAS
TEXAS
HOUSTON

OKLAHOMA

MONTERREY

MEXICO

GUADALAJARA

NEW MEXICO
Rio Grande

ARIZONA
PHOENIX

LOS ANGELES
SAN DIEGO
MEXICALI

Gulf of California

North America's first
European settlers
lived in New England
in the northeastern
United States. The
region is known for
its picturesque small-
town churches and
for its forests, where
the trees turn brilliant
colors in the autumn.

NORTH AMERICA

NORTH AMERICA includes Canada, the
United States, Mexico, Central America,
and the Caribbean islands, as well as the
largest island in the world, Greenland. In
the sparsely populated north, the thick
Arctic ice gives way to the barren tundra of
northern Canada. The Rocky Mountains
run down from Alaska to Mexico, while the
forested Appalachians dominate the eastern
United States. In the fertile lowlands of the
Mississippi basin and the eastern seaboard,
farms produce huge amounts of crops such
as corn and wheat. Further south are the
hot, dry deserts of southwestern United
States and Mexico.

Most people in North America are
descendants of settlers from other parts of
the world, the first of whom, the
Europeans, arrived in the 16th century.
Many Native American peoples lost their
lands and their lives to the new arrivals.
Today, the small groups of Native Americans
that remain have their own territories.
Many, especially the Inuit of northern
Canada, still follow a traditional way of life.

FACTFILE

Brightly colored wooden totem poles have been carved for generations by families of Native Americans on the northwest coast of Canada. The images depict the family's history, and which clan they belong to.

 ## CANADA

Area 3,845,000 sq mile (9,958,319 km²) **Population** 31,006,347 **Capital** Ottawa (population 1,010,288) **Languages** English, French **Religions** Roman Catholic 47%, Protestant 25%, other 28% **Currency** Canadian dollar **Highest point** Mount Logan 19,850 ft. (6,050 m) **Main industries** Wood and paper, metals, food, cars, chemicals, petroleum, telecommunications

 ## UNITED STATES

Area 3,619,000 sq mile (9,372,614 km²) **Population** 272,639,608 **Capital** Washington, D.C. **Languages** English, Spanish **Religions** Protestant 56%, Roman Catholic 28%, Jewish 2%, other 14% **Currency** U.S. dollar **Highest point** Mount McKinley, Alaska, 20,320 ft (6,194 m) **Main industries** Aircraft, cars, chemicals, computers, petroleum, steel, telecommunications, timber **Major cities** New York (16,332,000), Los Angeles (15,302,275), Chicago (8,526,804), Washington, D.C. (7,051,495), San Francisco (6,513,322)

 ## MEXICO

Area 761,600 sq miles (1,972,547 km²) **Population** 100,294,036 **Capital** Mexico City (pop. 23,913,000) **Language** Spanish **Religions** Roman Catholic 89%, Protestant 6%, other 5% **Currency** Mexican peso **Highest point** Citlaltépetl 18,700 ft (5,700 m) **Main industries** Petroleum, iron and steel, food, drink, cars, chemicals, tourism

Guatemala

CENTRAL AMERICA

Belize

Honduras

El Salvador

Nicaragua

Costa Rica

Panama

BELIZE
Area 8,867 sq mile (22,965 km²) **Population** 235,789 **Capital** Belmopan **Languages** English, Spanish

COSTA RICA
Area 19,580 sq mile (50,700 km²) **Population** 3,674,490 **Capital** San José **Language** Spanish

EL SALVADOR
Area 8,124 sq mile (21,041 km²) **Population** 5,839,079 **Capital** San Salvador **Language** Spanish

GUATEMALA
Area 42,040 sq mile (108,889 km²) **Population** 12,335,580 **Capital** Guatemala **Language** Spanish

HONDURAS
Area 43,280 sq mile (112,088 km²) **Population** 5,997,327 **Capital** Tegucigalpa **Language** Spanish

NICARAGUA
Area 50,190 sq mile (130,000 km²) **Population** 4,717,132 **Capital** Managua **Languages** Spanish, English

PANAMA
Area 29,160 sq mile (75,517 km²) **Population** 2,778,526 **Capital** Panama **Language** Spanish

Cuba

CARIBBEAN

Bahamas

Jamaica

Haiti

Dominican Republic

St. Kitts and Nevis

Antigua and Barbuda

Dominica

St. Lucia

St. Vincent

Barbados

Grenada

Trinidad and Tobago

ANGUILLA
Area 35.14 sq miles (91 km²) **Population** 11,510 **Capital** The Valley **Language** English

ANTIGUA AND BARBUDA
Area 171 sq miles (442 km²) **Population** 64,426 **Capital** St. John's **Language** English

BAHAMAS
Area 5,382 sq miles (13,939 km²) **Population** 283,705 **Capital** Nassau **Language** English

BARBADOS
Area 166 sq miles (430 km²) **Population** 259,191 **Capital** Bridgetown **Language** English

BERMUDA
Area 20.5 sq miles (53 km²) **Population** 62,472 **Capital** Hamilton **Language** English

BRITISH VIRGIN ISLANDS
Area 59 sq miles (153 km²) **Population** 19,156 **Capital** Road Town **Language** English

CUBA
Area 42,800 sq miles (110,860 km²) **Population** 11,096,395 **Capital** Havana **Language** Spanish

DOMINICA
Area 289.6 sq miles (750 km²) **Population** 64,881 **Capital** Roseau **Languages** English, Creole

DOMINICAN REPUBLIC
Area 18,700 sq miles (48,422 km²) **Population** 8,129,734 **Capital** Santo Domingo **Language** Spanish

GRENADA
Area 133.2 sq miles (345 km²) **Population** 97,008 **Capital** St. George's **Languages** English, French patois

GUADELOUPE
Area 689.9 sq miles (1779 km²) **Population** 420,943 **Capital** Basse-Terre **Languages** French, Creole

HAITI
Area 10,710 sq miles (27,750 km²) **Population** 6,884,264 **Capital** Port-au-Prince **Languages** French, Creole

JAMAICA
Area 4,244 sq miles (10,991 km²) **Population** 2,652,443 **Capital** Kingston **Language** English

MARTINIQUE
Area 425.5 sq miles (1102 km²) **Population** 411,539 **Capital** Fort-de-France **Languages** French, Creole

MONTSERRAT
Area 39.4 sq miles (102 km²) **Population** 12,853 **Capital** Plymouth **Language** English

NETHERLANDS ANTILLES
Area 309 sq miles (800 km²) **Population** 207,827 **Capital** Willemstad **Languages** Dutch, Papiamento

PUERTO RICO
Area 3,459 sq miles (8959 km²) **Population** 3,887,652 **Capital** San Juan **Languages** Spanish, English

ST. KITTS AND NEVIS
Area 101 sq miles (262 km²) **Population** 42,838 **Capital** Basseterre **Language** English

ST. LUCIA
Area 238 sq miles (616 km²) **Population** 154,020 **Capital** Castries **Languages** English, French patois

ST. VINCENT AND THE GRENADINES
Area 150 sq miles (388 km²) **Population** 120,519 **Capital** Kingstown **Language** English

TRINIDAD AND TOBAGO
Area 1,980 sq miles (5127 km²) **Population** 1,102,096 **Capital** Port of Spain **Languages** English, French, Spanish, Hindi, Chinese

U.S. VIRGIN ISLANDS
Area 137 sq miles (355 km²) **Population** 119,827 **Capital** Charlotte Amalie **Languages** English, Spanish, Creole

UNITED STATES

THE UNITED STATES stretches from the Atlantic Ocean in the east to the Pacific Ocean in the west. Numbered among its 50 states are Alaska, which lies to the northwest of Canada, and the Pacific islands of Hawaii.

Running down the northeastern side of the United States are the densely forested Appalachian Mountains. To their northwest lie the Great Lakes, vast inland seas that were gouged out by glaciers during the Ice Age and filled by their meltwaters. To the east lie the coastal lowlands, where great cities such as New York, Boston, and Washington, D.C., have grown up.

The famous symbol of San Francisco, the Golden Gate bridge spans the entrance to San Francisco Bay. It carries cars and pedestrians for 1.68 miles (2.7 km) across the water.

Covering the central belt of the United States is a vast, flat area of farmland. In the northern part, crops such as wheat and corn are grown, while cotton, tobacco, and nuts are cultivated further south. The vast Mississippi River cuts through several of the midwestern states, dividing the United States in two.

West of the high Rocky Mountains, the climate is drier, and the landscape more rugged. Wide areas of hot desert stretch across the southwestern states of Nevada and Arizona. Near the west coast, the climate becomes milder. Rich farmland nestles among the mountain ranges of California and the northwestern states.

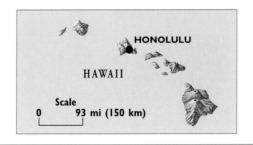

Before the first settlers arrived from Europe, the Native Americans were the only inhabitants of the United States. Today, Americans can trace their ancestors from all parts of the world. Many black Americans are the descendents of slaves brought over from Africa in the 17th and 18th centuries.

New Orleans, in the southern state of Louisiana, is the home of jazz and blues music. This originated from the songs of the early black population.

The Gateway Arch stands on the bank of the Mississippi River in St. Louis, Missouri. At 630 feet (192 m) high, it is the highest monument in the world. It was built in 1965, to symbolize the "Gateway to the West." In the 19th century, many people traveled west from St. Louis to begin a new life in Oregon and California.

Scale
0   249 mi (400 km)

ARCTIC OCEAN

Ellesmere Island

Banks I.

Melville I.

DAWSON

Victoria Island

BAFFIN BAY

NORTHWEST TERRITORIES

Baffin Island

YUKON

NUNAVUT

Great Bear Lake

Hudson Strait

YELLOWKNIFE

Ungava Peninsula

Great Slave Lake

LABRADOR

Scale
0   310 mi (500 km)

HUDSON BAY

BRITISH COLUMBIA

ALBERTA

MANITOBA

NEWFOUNDLAND

EDMONTON

L. Winnipeg

ST. JOHN'S

SASKATCHEWAN

CALGARY

QUÉBEC

Gulf of St. Lawrence

VANCOUVER

ONTARIO

PRINCE EDWARD I.

REGINA

NEW BRUNSWICK

HALIFAX

WINNIPEG

QUÉBEC

NOVA SCOTIA

L. Superior

MONTRÉAL

L. Huron

OTTAWA

TORONTO

L. Ontario

CANADA

ALTHOUGH larger in size than the United States, Canada has a much smaller population than its neighbor. Most of the country is covered with vast coniferous forests, mountains, and lakes, where bears, wolves, cougars, and moose are abundant. In the far north, and on the Arctic islands, the ground is permanently frozen. On this barren land, known as the tundra, plants grow only in the short summer.

Some native peoples, including the Inuit, live in the icy northern territories, but most Canadians live in the south, near the border with the United States. The largest cities are located in the east. Further west, in the provinces of Alberta, Saskatchewan, and Manitoba, lies a wide expanse of fertile, low-lying land known as the Great Plains, or prairies, where most of Canada's wheat crop is grown. The western part of Canada is dominated by mountain ranges, including the Rocky Mountains, which stretch on south across the United States.

Grain from the fertile prairies is stored in grain elevators before being distributed around Canada and abroad.

In the 16th century, the first European settlers arrived in Canada from both France and Great Britain. French and English are still the official languages spoken today. Most French-speaking Canadians live in the province of Québec, and many wish to see it declared a separate country.

MEXICO AND CENTRAL AMERICA

MEXICO and the countries that make up Central America form a link between North and South America. Mexico is a mountainous country, with desert in the north, tropical forest in the south and a central plateau of fertile land. Its cities suffer from overcrowding and pollution.

Central America is a mainly agricultural area. Bananas and coffee are grown, and cattle are raised. There is a constant threat of volcanoes, earthquakes, and hurricanes.

The first European settlers of this region were Spanish. They controlled the land for hundreds of years. Most Mexicans and Central Americans speak Spanish today.

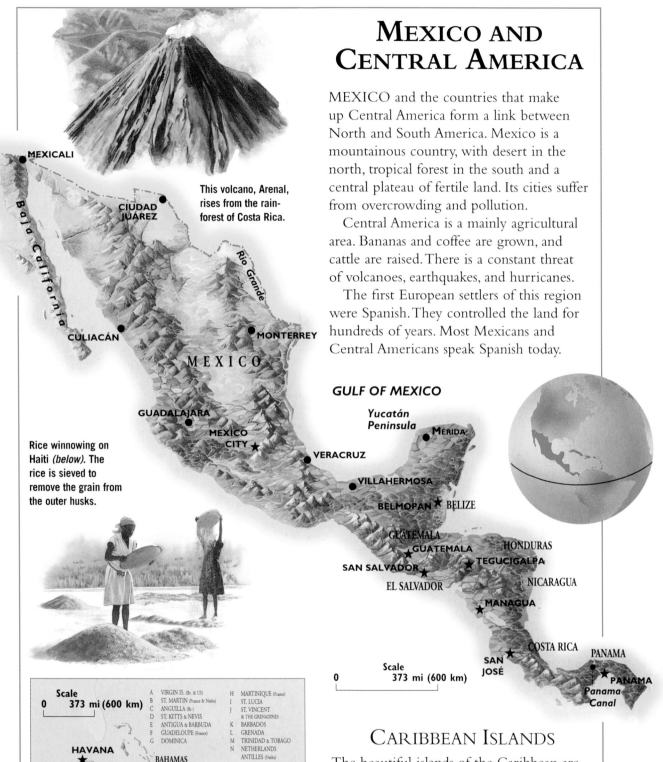

This volcano, Arenal, rises from the rain-forest of Costa Rica.

Rice winnowing on Haiti *(below)*. The rice is sieved to remove the grain from the outer husks.

GULF OF MEXICO

MEXICALI

CIUDAD JUÁREZ

Baja California

Rio Grande

CULIACÁN

MONTERREY

MEXICO

GUADALAJARA

MEXICO CITY ★

VERACRUZ

Yucatán Peninsula

MÉRIDA

VILLAHERMOSA

BELMOPAN ★ BELIZE

GUATEMALA
GUATEMALA ★

HONDURAS

SAN SALVADOR ★
EL SALVADOR

TEGUCIGALPA ★

NICARAGUA

MANAGUA ★

COSTA RICA

SAN JOSÉ ★

PANAMA

PANAMA ★
Panama Canal

Scale
0   373 mi (600 km)

CARIBBEAN ISLANDS

The beautiful islands of the Caribbean are popular tourist resorts. They also export crops such as sugar, bananas, and coffee. Volcanic eruptions and frequent hurricanes are a constant threat to the islanders. Many Caribbean people are descended from black African slaves. Their cultures are a mixture of African and European traditions.

Scale
0   373 mi (600 km)

A	VIRGIN IS. (Br. & US)	H	MARTINIQUE (France)
B	ST. MARTIN (France & Neths)	I	ST. LUCIA
C	ANGUILLA (Br.)	J	ST. VINCENT & THE GRENADINES
D	ST. KITTS & NEVIS		
E	ANTIGUA & BARBUDA	K	BARBADOS
F	GUADELOUPE (France)	L	GRENADA
G	DOMINICA	M	TRINIDAD & TOBAGO
		N	NETHERLANDS ANTILLES (Neths)

HAVANA ★

BAHAMAS

CUBA

DOMINICAN REPUBLIC

JAMAICA
KINGSTON ★

HAITI

SANTO DOMINGO ★

PUERTO RICO (US)

C
E
A
B D
F G
H
J I K
L
M
N

CARIBBEAN SEA

SOUTH AMERICA

SOUTH AMERICA is a continent of extremes. The world's longest mountain range, the Andes, stretches along the west coast. Between the snow-capped mountains lies a high, cold, and windswept plain called the altiplano. Between the Andes and the Pacific Ocean coast is the Atacama Desert, the driest place on earth. Rain may not fall here for hundreds of years at a time.

In the north, most people live near the Caribbean coast or in the mountains. Further inland, the vast rain forests of the Amazon basin dominate. The Amazon River originates in the Andes, and winds its way eastward through Peru and Brazil before reaching the Atlantic Ocean.

To the east of the Amazon rain forest lie the Brazilian Highlands. Further south are wide areas of fertile grasslands, known as pampas, which cover parts of Argentina and Uruguay. In the extreme south of

Argentina, grasslands give way to the dry, bleak scrublands of Patagonia. The southern Andes is an region of glaciers and volcanoes, breaking up into bleak, rocky islands at its tip.

Many people in South America are descended from Europeans, especially the Spanish and Portuguese, who began to arrive during the 15th century. Most South American people today still speak these languages. Others are descendents of African slaves brought over by the Europeans. The numbers of native peoples of South America fell dramatically after the arrival of the Europeans, but some still live in the mountains and the rain forest, keeping their own languages and traditions.

A Chilean boy. Many people living in South America today are of mixed European and native Indian descent. They are known as mestizos.

This scarlet macaw is one of the many birds of the rain forest.

The destruction of the rain forests does not only mean a loss of habitat for plants and animals. The bare landscape that is left also leads to soil erosion, while some scientists think that the loss of so many trees may affect the world's climate.

AMAZON RAIN FOREST

The Amazon basin is the largest area of rain forest in the world. Many kinds of plants and animals live there, and new species are constantly being discovered. The mighty Amazon River and its tributaries flow through the forest, providing a vital

transportation route and source of food for the native peoples who live in forest villages. A few of these peoples still follow a traditional way of life, hunting, fishing, and growing crops. Many also take advantage of modern technology, such as engines for their boats.

Today, the rain forest is disappearing at an alarming rate, because of logging for the timber industry, roadbuilding, and clearing space for cattle farming or crop planting. The poor-quality rain forest soil means that it cannot support grazing or crops for long before the farmers must move on to new areas. So even more of the forest is lost.

Some rain forest peoples live in one part of the forest for a while, where they hunt and grow basic crops, and then move on to another site to give the soil a chance to recover. As more and more of the forest is cut down, their homelands are depleted. They have also suffered from persecution and illness as outsiders have moved into the forest.

FACTFILE

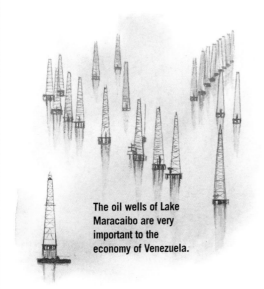

The oil wells of Lake Maracaibo are very important to the economy of Venezuela.

NORTHERN

Colombia

Venezuela

Guyana

Surinam

Ecuador

Peru

Bolivia

BOLIVIA
Area 424,200 sq miles (1,098,581 km²)
Population 7,982,850 **Capitals** La Paz, Sucre
Languages Spanish, Quechua, Aymara
COLOMBIA
Area 440,800 sq miles (1,141,748 km²) **Pop.**
39,309,422 **Capital** Bogotá **Language** Spanish
Religions Roman Catholic 95%, other 5%
ECUADOR
Area 105,000 sq miles (272,045 km²) **Population**
12,562,496 **Capital** Quito **Languages** Spanish,
Quechua
FRENCH GUIANA
Area 35,140 sq miles (91,000 km²) **Pop.** 167,982
Capital Cayenne **Languages** French, Creole
GUYANA
Area 83,000 sq miles (214,969 km²) **Population**
705,156 **Capital** Georgetown **Languages**
English, Hindi, Urdu

PERU
Area 496,200 sq miles (1,285,216 km²)
Population 26,624,582 **Capital** Lima
Languages Spanish, Quechua, Aymara **Religions**
Roman Catholic 89%, other 11%
SURINAM
Area 63,040 sq miles (163,265 km²) **Population**
431,156 **Capital** Paramaribo **Languages** Dutch,
Hindi, Javanese
VENEZUELA
Area 352,100 sq miles (912,050 km²) **Population**
23,203,466 **Capital** Caracas **Language** Spanish
Religions Roman Catholic 96%, other 4%

BRAZIL

Area 3,286,500 sq miles (8,511,996 km²)
Population 171,853,126 **Capital** Brasília
Language Portuguese **Religions** Roman
Catholic 90%, other 10% **Currency** Real **Highest
point** Pico da Neblina 9,888 ft (3,014 m) **Main
industries** Cars, aircraft, machinery, textiles,
clothing, chemicals, steel

A Native American woman steers a boat on the highest navigable lake in the world, Lake Titicaca *(right),* which stretches between Peru and Bolivia. The boat is made from tough, tightly bundled reeds. People also live on floating island villages in the lake, made from thickly piled reeds. When the reeds at the bottom rot away, more layers are piled up on top.

Rio de Janeiro, or "January River" *(below),* lies on the coast of Brazil. It was named after the month in which Portuguese explorer Goncalo Coelho sailed into its bay in 1503. A great city has since grown up beneath the famous Sugar Loaf mountain. In the 19th century, Rio de Janeiro was an important port trading gold and diamonds mined in the interior of the country. Today, poverty-stricken shantytowns cluster on the outskirts, crowded with people desperate for work.

SOUTHERN

Chile

Paraguay

Uruguay

Argentina

ARGENTINA
Area 1,068,000 sq miles (2,766,889 km²)
Population 36,737,664 **Capital** Buenos Aires
Language Spanish **Religions** Roman Catholic
90%, Protestant 2%, other 8% **Currency**
Argentine peso

CHILE
Area 292,100 sq miles (756,626 km²)
Population 14,973,843 **Capital** Santiago
Language Spanish **Religions** Roman Catholic
89%, Protestant 11%

PARAGUAY
Area 157,000 sq miles (406,752 km²) **Population**
5,434,096 **Capital** Asunción **Languages** Spanish,
Guarani **Religions** Roman Catholic 90%,
Protestant 10%

URUGUAY
Area 68,037 sq miles (176,215 km²) **Pop.**
3,284,841 **Capital** Montevideo **Language**
Spanish **Religions** Roman Catholic 66%,
Protestant 2%, Jewish 2%, other 30%

SOUTH AMERICA

VENEZUELA, the Guianas (Guyana, Surinam, and French Guiana), and Brazil are rich in natural resources such as oil, bauxite, silver, and other minerals. Brazil also produces coffee, sugar, and fruit for export, while Guyana has large sugar plantations. Despite these resources, there is a great contrast in the distribution of wealth. A few people are very rich, while others live in poverty. The towns and cities are densely populated with people looking for work. Clusters of poor housing known as shantytowns, built from whatever materials can be found, sprawl around the edges of cities such as Rio de Janeiro and São Paulo.

Scale
373 mi (600 km)
0

This girl is a native of the Amazon rain forest. The few Amazon Indian tribes that still live in the forest rely on it for food, shelter, and medicines. Some build villages and grow crops while others are nomadic hunters.

CARIBBEAN SEA

MARACAIBO

CARACAS

Orinoco

V E N E Z U E L A

Guiana Highlands

G U Y A N A

GEORGETOWN

PARAMARIBO

CAYENNE

SURINAM

FRENCH GUIANA

BELÉM

Amazon

Negro

MANAUS

Japurá

Amazon

Madeira

Xingu

Tocantins

Brazilian Highlands

B R A Z I L

São Francisco

FORTALEZA

RECIFE

SALVADOR

BRASÍLIA ★

MEDELLÍN

BOGOTÁ

CALI

COLOMBIA

Andes Mountains

QUITO

ECUADOR

GUAYAQUIL

IQUITOS

Marañón

Ucayali

P E R U

Andes Mountains

LIMA ★

TRUJILLO

CUZCO

L. Titicaca

B O L I V I A

LA PAZ ★

The northern Andean countries of Colombia, Ecuador, Peru, and Bolivia are also rich in minerals. Fertile farming land is scarce, so farmers have cut terraces into the hillsides to form level fields. Cotton, sugarcane, coffee, and bananas are grown in the warm lowlands, while cereals and potatoes grow in higher, cooler regions. Economic problems and political unrest have caused poverty in these countries.

Further south is the long, narrow country of Chile. Mining, especially copper, is very important in the Andes Mountains, while the valleys are fertile, producing cereals, fruits, and vines. East of the Andes are the open grasslands, known as pampas, of Argentina and Uruguay. Here, millions of cattle and sheep graze on vast ranches. They are exported for their meat and wool. Chile, Uruguay, and Argentina all have modern cities and a high standard of living. The Gran Chaco, a dry, scrubland plain, covers much of northwest Paraguay. Cattle are farmed and cotton grown in the more fertile south and east. Paraguay has the world's largest hydroelectric project, the Itaipú Dam on the Paraná river.

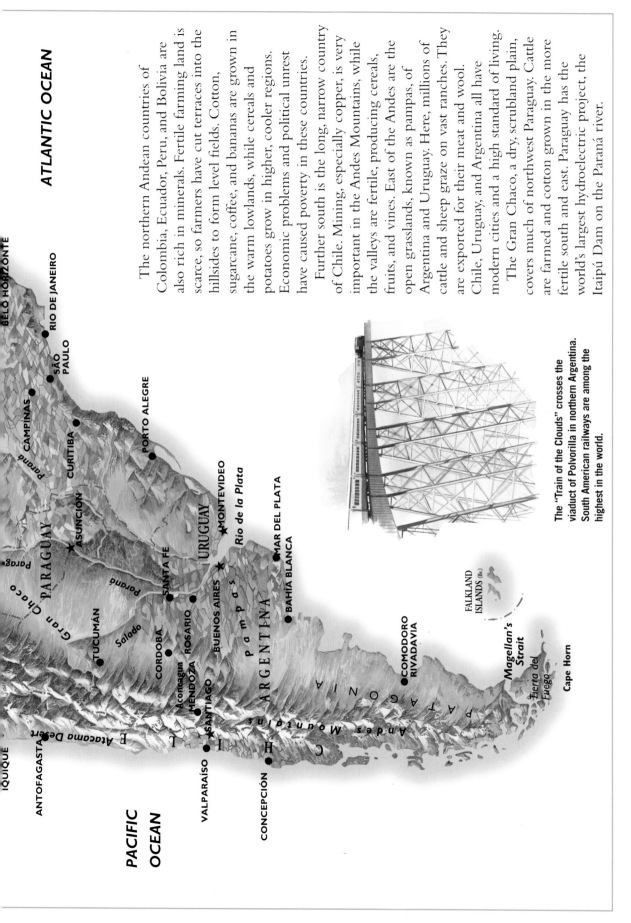

The "Train of the Clouds" crosses the viaduct of Polvorilla in northern Argentina. South American railways are among the highest in the world.

ATLANTIC OCEAN

BELO HORIZONTE

RIO DE JANEIRO

SÃO PAULO

Paraná

CAMPINAS

CURITIBA

PORTO ALEGRE

ASUNCIÓN

PARAGUAY

Paraguay

★MONTEVIDEO

Río de la Plata

URUGUAY

SANTA FE

Paraná

Gran Chaco

TUCUMÁN

Salado

CÓRDOBA

ROSARIO

BUENOS AIRES

Pampas

MAR DEL PLATA

BAHÍA BLANCA

Aconcagua

MENDOZA

SANTIAGO

A R G E N T I N A

FALKLAND ISLANDS (Br.)

COMODORO RIVADAVIA

P A T A G O N I A

Magellan's Strait

Tierra del Fuego

Cape Horn

Andes Mountains

Atacama Desert

IQUIQUE

ANTOFAGASTA

C H I L E

VALPARAÍSO

CONCEPCIÓN

PACIFIC OCEAN

EUROPE

EUROPE is a dense patchwork of nations. The continent is actually part of a single landmass that also includes Asia, but there are also a number of islands. A large part of Russia and a small part of Turkey are also included within Europe.

In the far north, Europe borders the Arctic Ocean. Frozen tundra merges into the vast coniferous forests of Russia and Scandinavia. The Gulf Stream, a warm ocean current, gives the northwestern countries a mild, wet climate. Central Europe and Russia have hot summers but cold winters. To the south, beyond the mountain ranges of the Pyrenees and the Alps, lie the sunny Mediterranean lands.

Europe is, for the most part, densely populated. Waterways and road and rail networks link its major cities. Much of its land is under cultivation or pasture. Only a few large areas of uninhabited land remain in the north.

Compared to other parts of the world, European countries are wealthy, though the west is generally more prosperous. Through history, conflicts have flared between and within countries. Several have split into smaller, independent nations in recent years.

Europe has a long history, and many old buildings from hundreds of years ago are still standing today. These buildings in Bruges, Belgium (below), date back to medieval times.

People who originate from many different parts of the world now live in Europe. Countries such as England, France, and Spain once ruled much of America, Africa, and Asia. Many people from these continents have now settled in Europe, giving it a rich variety of cultures.

NORWAY

SWEDEN

FINLAND

MURMANSK

White Sea

ARKHANGELSK

RUSSIA

L.Onega

PERM

IDHEIM

L.Ladoga

TURKU **HELSINKI**

ST. PETERSBURG

STOCKHOLM

TALLINN
ESTONIA

ÖTEBORG

BALTIC SEA

RIGA
LATVIA

LITHUANIA
VILNIUS

RUSSIA

NIZHNIY NOVGOROD

MOSCOW

SAMARA

PENHAGEN

GDANSK
KALININGRAD

MINSK

BELARUS

VORONEZH

RLIN
SZCZECIN

POLAND

WARSAW

Vistula

WROCŁAW

KIEV
Dnieper

UKRAINE

KHARKIV

VOLGOGRAD
Don

Volga

ASTRAKHAN

PRAGUE
CH REPUBLIC
KATOWICE

L'VIV

DNIPROPETROVSK

DONETSK

ROSTOV

Caspian Sea

SLOVAKIA

CHERNIVTSI

Dniester

MOLDOVA

IENNA

BRATISLAVA

BUDAPEST

HUNGARY

CHISINAU

ODESA

KRASNODAR

STRIA

OVENIA
ZAGREB

CROATIA

ROMANIA

SOCHI

BUCHAREST

Danube

BOSNIA
BELGRADE

SARAJEVO

YUGOSLAVIA

BLACK SEA

BULGARIA

NAPLES

TIRANE
ALBANIA

SOFIA

SKOPJE
MACEDONIA

ISTANBUL

T U R K E Y

Adriatic Sea

THESSALONIKI

Aegean Sea

GREECE

Sicily

ATHENS

ALTA

Crete

CYPRUS
NICOSIA

★ Capital city

Scale

0 ───────── 373 mi (600 km)

Religious buildings are often
some of the grandest that
survive today. This is the
Alexander Nevski Cathedral in
Sofia, the capital of Bulgaria.

FACTFILE I

The west coast of Scotland *(above)*, in the United Kingdom, is an area of mountains and sea lochs.

NORTHERN

Iceland

Norway

Sweden

Finland

Denmark

UK

Ireland

Belgium

Netherlands

Luxembourg

IRELAND
Area 27,137 sq miles (70,283 km²) **Population** 3,632,944 **Capital** Dublin **Languages** English, Irish **Religions** Roman Catholic 93%, Protestant 3%, other 4%

LUXEMBOURG
Area 998.5 sq miles (2,586 km²) **Population** 429,080 **Capital** Luxembourg **Languages** German, Letzeburgesch, French **Religions** Roman Catholic 97%, other 3%

NETHERLANDS
Area 13,102 sq miles (33,936 km²) **Population** 15,807,641 **Capitals** Amsterdam, The Hague **Language** Dutch **Religions** Roman Catholic 36%, Protestant 27%, Muslim 2%, other 35%

NORWAY
Area 125,050 sq miles (323,877 km²) **Pop.** 4,438,547 **Capital** Oslo **Language** Norwegian **Religions** Protestant 88%, other 12%

The castle of Vianden *(below)* lies among the wooded hills of Luxembourg.

BELGIUM
Area 11,780 sq miles (30,519 km²) **Population** 10,182,034 **Capital** Brussels **Languages** Dutch (Flemish), French, German **Religions** Roman Catholic 75%, Protestant 15%, Muslim 3%, other 7%

DENMARK
Area 16,640 sq miles (43,093 km²) **Population** 5,356,845 **Capital** Copenhagen **Language** Danish **Religions** Protestant 90%, other 10%

FINLAND
Area 130,600 sq miles (338,145 km²) **Population** 5,158,372 **Capital** Helsinki **Languages** Finnish, Swedish **Religions** Protestant 89%, other 11%

ICELAND
Area 39,770 sq miles (103,000 km²) **Population** 272,512 **Capital** Reykjavik **Language** Icelandic **Religions** Protestant 96%, other 4%

SWEDEN
Area 173,732 sq miles (449,964 km²) **Pop.** 8,886,738 **Capital** Stockholm **Languages** Swedish, Finnish, Lappish **Religions** Protestant 94%, Roman Catholic 2%, other 4%

UNITED KINGDOM
Area 93,643 sq miles (242,533 km²) **Pop.** 59,113,439 **Capital** London **Languages** English, Welsh **Religions** Protestant 51%, Roman Catholic 9%, Muslim 3%, other 37% **Highest point** Ben Nevis 4,406 ft (1,343 m) **Main industries** Cars, machinery, aircraft, chemicals, textiles, tourism, banking

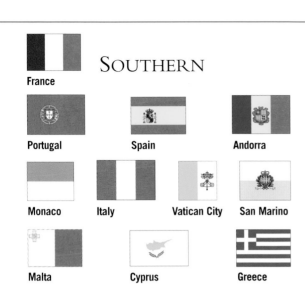

SOUTHERN

France

Portugal Spain Andorra

Monaco Italy Vatican City San Marino

Malta Cyprus Greece

ANDORRA
Area 181 sq miles (468 km²) **Population** 65,786
Capital Andorra **Languages** Catalan, French, Spanish

CYPRUS
Area 3,572 sq miles (9251 km²) **Pop.** 754,064
Capital Nicosia **Languages** Greek, Turkish, English

FRANCE
Area 210,026 sq miles (543,965 km²) **Pop.** 58,978,172 **Capital** Paris **Language** French
Religions Roman Catholic 90%, other 10%
Main industries Cars, chemicals, machinery, steel, aircraft, electronics, food, tourism

GREECE
Area 50,949 sq miles (131,957 km²) **Pop.** 10,707,135 **Capital** Athens **Language** Greek
Religions Orthodox 98%, other 2%

ITALY
Area 116,324 sq miles (301,277 km²) **Population** 56,735,130 **Capital** Rome **Language** Italian
Religion Roman Catholic 100% **Main industries** Clothing, chemicals, cars, ceramics, food, tourism

MALTA
Area 122 sq miles (316 km²) **Population** 376,513
Capital Valletta **Languages** Maltese, English, Italian

MONACO
Area .77 sq miles (2 km²) **Population** 32,149
Capital Monaco **Language** French

PORTUGAL
Area 35,672 sq miles (92,389 km²) **Population** 9,918,040 **Capital** Lisbon **Language** Portuguese
Religions Roman Catholic 97%, Protestant 1%, other 2%

SAN MARINO
Area 23.36 sq miles (60.5 km²) **Population** 25,061 **Capital** San Marino **Language** Italian

SPAIN
Area 194,897 sq miles (504,782 km²) **Population** 39,167,744 **Capital** Madrid **Languages** Spanish, Catalan, Basque, Galician **Religions** Roman Catholic 99%, other 1% **Main industries** Cars, clothing, shoes, chemicals, metals, food and drink, tourism

VATICAN CITY
Area .17 sq miles (0.44 km²) **Population** 850

The fifteen towers of San Gimignano (below), in Tuscany, central Italy, are all that remain of 72 built 600 years ago.

FACTFILE II

A typical Swiss house

CENTRAL

Germany   Austria   Switzerland

Liechtenstein   Slovenia   Hungary

Czech Republic   Slovakia   Poland

AUSTRIA
Area 32,378 sq miles (83,859 km²) **Population** 8,139,299 **Capital** Vienna **Language** German **Religions** Roman Catholic 85%, other 15%

CZECH REPUBLIC
Area 30,450 sq miles (78,864 km²) **Population** 10,280,513 **Capital** Prague **Language** Czech **Religions** Roman Catholic 39%, Protestant 4% other 57%

GERMANY
Area 137,782 sq miles (356,854 km²) **Pop.** 82,087,361 **Capital** Berlin **Language** German **Religions** Protestant 45%, Roman Catholic 37%, other 18% **Highest point** Zugspitze 9,718 ft (2,962 m) **Main industries** Cars, machinery, chemicals, electronic goods, banking

HUNGARY
Area 35,919 sq miles (93,030 km²) **Population** 10,186,372 **Capital** Budapest **Language** Hungarian **Religions** Roman Catholic 68%, Protestant 25%, other 7%

LIECHTENSTEIN
Area 61.78 sq miles (160 km²) **Pop.** 32,057 **Capital** Vaduz **Language** German

POLAND
Area 120,728 sq miles (312,683 km²) **Pop.** 38,608,929 **Capital** Warsaw **Language** Polish **Religions** Roman Catholic 95%, other 5%

SLOVAKIA
Area 18,933 sq miles (49,035 km²) **Population** 5,396,193 **Capital** Bratislava **Languages** Slovak, Hungarian, Czech **Religions** Roman Catholic 64%, Protestant 8%, other 28%

SLOVENIA
Area 7,819 sq miles (20,251 km²) **Population** 1,970,570 **Capital** Ljubljana **Language** Slovene **Religions** Roman Catholic 96%, other 4%

SWITZERLAND
Area 15,943 sq miles (41,293 km²) **Population** 7,275,467 **Capital** Bern **Languages** German, French, Italian **Religions** Roman Catholic 48%, Protestant 44%, other 8%

Prague Castle *(below)*, **known to the Czechs as Hradcany, overlooks the city from the top of a hill.**

Croatia

BALKANS

EASTERN

Bosnia

Yugoslavia

Macedonia

Lithuania

Latvia

Estonia

Albania

Bulgaria

Romania

Belarus

Ukraine

Moldova

ALBANIA
Area 10,578 sq miles (27,398 km²) **Population** 3,364,571 **Capital** Tiranë **Language** Albanian
BOSNIA AND HERZEGOVINA
Area 19,741 sq miles (51,129 sq km **Population** 3,482,495 **Capital** Sarajevo **Language** Serbo-Croat
BULGARIA
Area 42,855 sq miles (110,994 km²) **Population** 8,194,722 **Capital** Sofia **Languages** Bulgarian, Turkish, Macedonian
CROATIA
Area 21,829 sq miles (56,538 km²) **Population** 4,676,865 **Capital** Zagreb **Language** Serbo-Croat
MACEDONIA
Area 9,928 sq miles (25,713 km²) **Pop.** 2,022,604 **Capital** Skopje **Languages** Macedonian, Albanian
ROMANIA
Area 91,699 sq miles (237,500 km²) **Population** 22,334,312 **Capital** Bucharest **Languages** Romanian, Hungarian, German
YUGOSLAVIA
Area 39,518 sq miles (102,350 km²) **Population** 11,206,847 **Capital** Belgrade **Languages** Serbo-Croat, Albanian, Hungarian

BELARUS
Area 80,155 sq miles (207,600 km²) **Pop.** 10,401,784 **Capital** Minsk **Language** Belorussian
ESTONIA
Area 17,423 sq miles (45,125 km²) **Population** 1,408,523 **Capital** Tallinn **Languages** Estonian, Russian
LATVIA
Area 25,054 sq miles (64,589 km²) **Population** 2,353,874 **Capital** Riga **Languages** Latvian, Russian
LITHUANIA
Area 25,174 sq miles (65,200 km²) **Population** 3,584,966 **Capital** Vilnius **Languages** Lithuanian, Russian, Polish, Belorussian
MOLDOVA
Area 13,012 sq miles (33,700 km²) **Population** 4,460,838 **Capital** Chisinau **Languages** Romanian (Moldovan), Ukrainian, Russian
UKRAINE
Area 233,090 sq miles (603,700 km²) **Population** 49,811,174 **Capital** Kiev **Languages** Ukrainian, Russian

RUSSIA
Area 6,592,849 sq miles (17,075,400 km²) **Population** 146,393,569 **Capital** Moscow **Languages** Russian, 38 other languages **Religions** Russian Orthodox 75%, other 25% **Currency** Rouble **Highest point** Elbrus 18,511 ft (5,642 m) **Main industries** Petroleum, machines, chemicals, steel, aircraft, weapons, trains, textiles **Major cities** Moscow (8,663,142), St. Petersburg (4,827,538), Novosibirsk (1,401,100), Nizhniy Novgorod (1,391,250), Yekaterinburg (1,322,950)

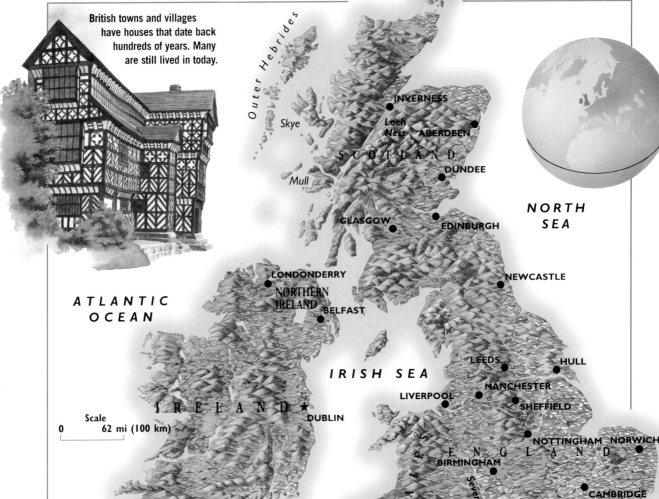

British towns and villages have houses that date back hundreds of years. Many are still lived in today.

Orkney Is.

Outer Hebrides

Skye

INVERNESS

Loch Ness

ABERDEEN

Mull

S C O T L A N D

DUNDEE

GLASGOW

EDINBURGH

NORTH SEA

ATLANTIC OCEAN

LONDONDERRY

NORTHERN IRELAND

BELFAST

NEWCASTLE

IRISH SEA

LEEDS

HULL

LIVERPOOL

MANCHESTER

SHEFFIELD

I R E L A N D

DUBLIN

Scale
0   62 mi (100 km)

NOTTINGHAM   NORWICH

W A L E S   E N G L A N D

BIRMINGHAM

CAMBRIDGE

Severn

OXFORD

CORK

Thames

LONDON

CARDIFF

BRISTOL

Bristol Channel

SOUTHAMPTON

BRIGHTON

PLYMOUTH

E N G L I S H   C H A N N E L

BRITISH ISLES

THE BRITISH ISLES includes the large islands of Great Britain and Ireland, and many smaller islands. England, Scotland, Wales and Northern Ireland make up the United Kingdom. The rest of Ireland became independent in 1922. For many years conflict has divided the Catholic and Protestant people of Northern Ireland.

Mountains dominate the sparsely populated north of Scotland. Northern England and Wales also have large areas of uplands. Central and southern England are a dense mix of farmland, towns, and cities. Because of its mild, wet climate, Ireland is famous for its lush green landscape.

The United Kingdom was once dominated by heavy industries such as coal-mining and shipbuilding. Today, light industry such as plastics manufacture and electronics, as well as communications and financial services, have become important.

Once the hub of a worldwide empire, Britain still plays a leading role in inter-national affairs. Its language, English, is spoken as a second language all over the world, and is dominant on the Internet and other areas of international communication.

FRANCE

FRANCE shares borders with several other countries on its eastern side, but the north and west look onto the sea. In the south, the Pyrenees mountains separate France from Spain, while the Alps form a border with Italy in the east. The Mediterranean Sea gives the south coast its warm climate and makes it a popular destination for tourists.

Much of France, especially in the north, is strongly agricultural. Many large rivers wind across fertile, undulating plains. France exports large quantities of food and wine, famous for its quality. It also has modern manufacturing and chemical industries. Nuclear power provides much of the country's electricity supplies.

Most people in France are descended from ancient peoples including the Gauls, a central European tribe, and the Franks, after whom the country is named. More recently, people from France's former colonies in North Africa have made their homes in France.

Mont-Saint-Michel and its medieval abbey stand just off the coast of Normandy, in northern France. At high tide, the sea covers the road leading to it.

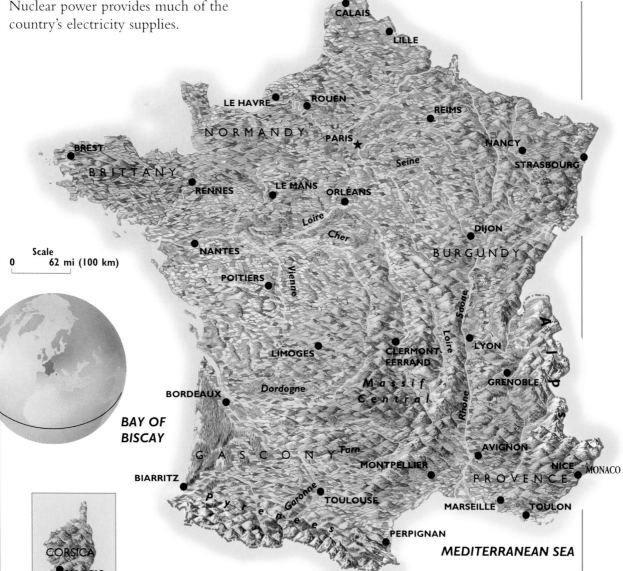

Scale
0   62 mi (100 km)

CALAIS
LILLE
LE HAVRE
ROUEN
REIMS
NORMANDY
PARIS ★
NANCY
STRASBOURG
Seine
BREST
BRITTANY
RENNES
LE MANS
ORLÉANS
Loire
Cher
DIJON
BURGUNDY
NANTES
POITIERS
Vienne
Saône
Loire
LYON
LIMOGES
CLERMONT-FERRAND
GRENOBLE
ALPS
BAY OF BISCAY
BORDEAUX
Dordogne
Massif Central
Rhône
GASCONY
Tarn
AVIGNON
MONTPELLIER
NICE
MONACO
BIARRITZ
Pyrenees
Garonne
TOULOUSE
PROVENCE
MARSEILLE
TOULON
PERPIGNAN
MEDITERRANEAN SEA

CORSICA
AJACCIO

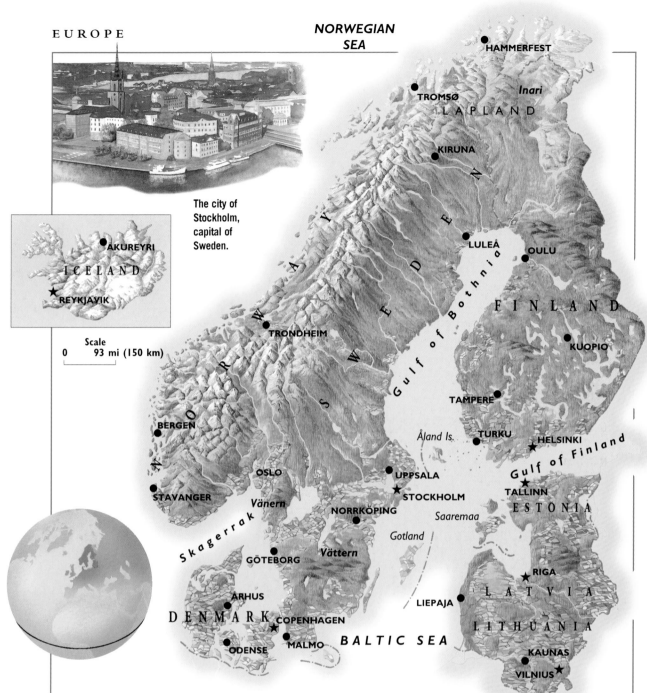

NORWEGIAN SEA

HAMMERFEST

TROMSØ Inari
LAPLAND

KIRUNA

LULEÅ OULU

FINLAND

TRONDHEIM KUOPIO

BERGEN TAMPERE

Åland Is. TURKU HELSINKI

OSLO UPPSALA Gulf of Finland

STAVANGER STOCKHOLM TALLINN

Vänern NORRKÖPING Saaremaa ESTONIA

Skagerrak Gotland

GÖTEBORG Vättern RIGA

ÅRHUS LIEPAJA LATVIA

DENMARK COPENHAGEN LITHUANIA

ODENSE MALMO BALTIC SEA KAUNAS

VILNIUS

Gulf of Bothnia

NORWAY SWEDEN

The city of
Stockholm,
capital of
Sweden.

AKUREYRI

ICELAND

REYKJAVIK

Scale
0   93 mi (150 km)

NORTHERN EUROPE

NORWAY, Sweden, and Denmark are
together known as Scandinavia. Along with
Finland and the volcanic island of Iceland,
they form the Nordic countries. Some parts
of Norway, Sweden, and Finland lie within
the Arctic Circle, where the sun never sets
in high summer, but never rises in the
depths of the long, cold winter.

Norway and Sweden are mountainous
countries, while Finland and Denmark are
low lying. Finland is covered with dense
coniferous forests and many lakes. In the

past, glaciers have carved out the many
inlets, or fjords, in Norway's coastline.

The Nordic countries are prosperous and
have low populations. They are important
producers of timber, and are also world
leaders in manufacturing. Denmark is also a
farming country, with many dairy and pig
farms.

The Baltic countries of Estonia, Latvia,
and Lithuania used to be part of the former
Soviet Union. Timber, fishing, and farming
are their most important industries.

GERMANY AND THE LOW COUNTRIES

AT THE CENTER of Europe lies Germany, with its neighbors Austria and Switzerland, and the "low countries" of Belgium, the Netherlands, and Luxembourg.

Germany is flat and fertile in the north and heavily forested in the hills of the central and southern areas. It is a wealthy country, and an industrial leader, producing cars, electrical goods, and chemicals for export all over the world.

The Alps rise in the south of Germany. Much of the area of Austria and Switzerland is taken up by Alpine peaks and valleys. These picturesque, prosperous countries also have modern industries.

The Brandenburg Gate in Berlin.

The Netherlands is famous for its dairy goods and fields of flowers. Belgium is a land of two regions: The north, Dutch-speaking Flanders, is mostly level farmland, while the south, French-speaking Wallonia is hilly, wooded country.

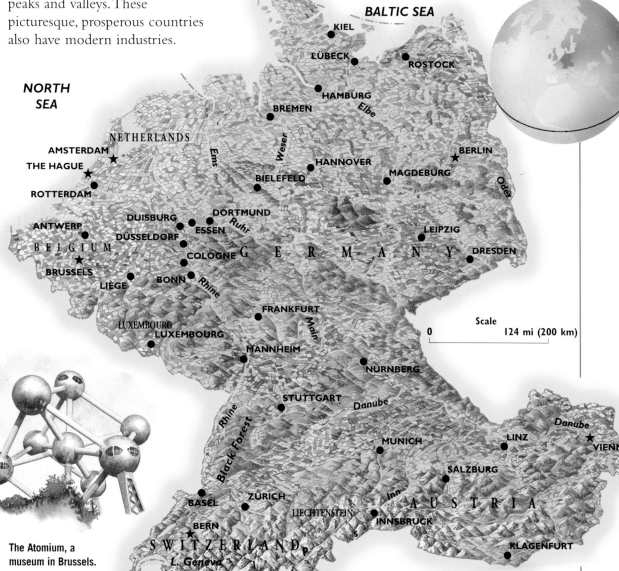

The Atomium, a museum in Brussels.

29

SPAIN AND PORTUGAL

THE IBERIAN PENINSULA, divided between the countries of Spain and Portugal, is separated from the rest of Europe by the Pyrenees mountains. The core of the peninsula is a plateau called the Meseta, a landscape of plains crossed by several mountain ranges.

Spain has four official languages—Galician, Catalan, Basque, as well as Spanish—and several dialects. The north of the country, Spain's industrial heartland, is cooler and wetter. Central Spain is much drier. Large areas are barren or given over to rough pasture for sheep and goats. Tourist resorts have grown up along the Mediterranean coast. Andalucia is famous for bullfighting, sherry, orange trees, and flamenco dancers.

Portugal has long held close ties with the sea. Famous for its explorers, Portuguese

The Luiz I bridge spans the River Douro at Porto, northern Portugal.

sailors founded colonies in Africa, Asia, and America more than 500 years ago. Today, farming and fishing are among the main industries—supplying the world with anchovies, sardines, shellfish, cork, and port, a sweet wine produced in the region near Porto. Along the drier south coast is the Algarve, popular with tourists.

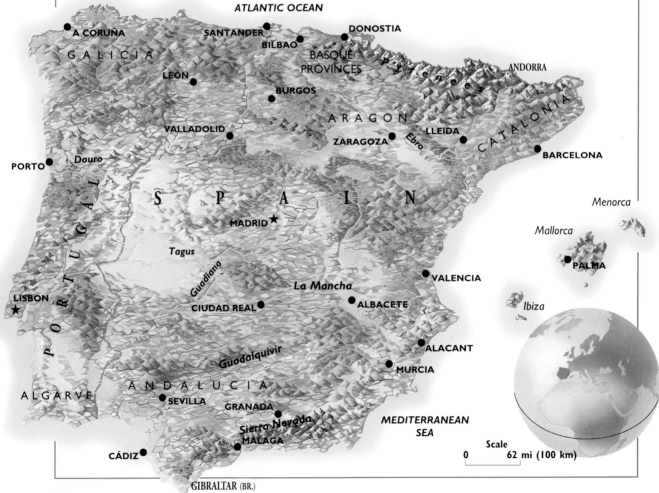

ATLANTIC OCEAN

A CORUÑA
SANTANDER
DONOSTIA
BILBAO
GALICIA
BASQUE PROVINCES
LEÓN
Pyrenees
ANDORRA
BURGOS
VALLADOLID
ARAGON
LLEIDA
CATALONIA
ZARAGOZA
Ebro
PORTO
Douro
BARCELONA
PORTUGAL
S P A I N
Menorca
MADRID
Mallorca
Tagus
PALMA
Guadiana
La Mancha
VALENCIA
LISBON
Ibiza
CIUDAD REAL
ALBACETE
Guadalquivir
ALACANT
MURCIA
ANDALUCIA
ALGARVE
SEVILLA
GRANADA
MEDITERRANEAN SEA
Sierra Nevada
MÁLAGA
CÁDIZ
Scale
0   62 mi (100 km)
GIBRALTAR (BR.)

BOLZANO

MILAN

TURIN

Po

GENOA

PARMA

Po

Adige

TRIESTE

VENICE

BOLOGNA

*ADRIATIC
SEA*

FLORENCE

Arno

LIVORNO

SAN MARINO

ANCONA

Elba

PERUGIA

Tiber

PESCARA

VATICAN CITY ★ ROME
STATE

SASSARI

SARDINIA

BARI

NAPLES *Vesuvius*

TARANTO

TYRRHENIAN SEA

CAGLIARI

Scale

0   62 mi (100 km)

Stromboli

MESSINA

PALERMO

Etna

S I C I L Y

CATANIA

*MEDITERRANEAN
SEA*

Venice was built on an island in a
lagoon. Instead of streets and cars,
there are canals and gondolas.

ITALY

SURROUNDED on three sides
by the Mediterranean Sea, Italy is
shaped like a boot about to kick a stone—
the island of Sicily. The Alps, including the
jagged, limestone Dolomites, form the
border in the north. Running the length of
the boot down to the toe are the thickly
wooded Apennines. Both Sicily and Sardinia
are rugged, hilly islands.

Italy also has three active volcanoes:
Vesuvius, Stromboli, and Etna. In A.D. 79,
Vesuvius erupted, burying the town of
Pompeii. The remains of a great Roman
civilization have since been uncovered.

Northern Italy is more prosperous than
the south, Sicily and Sardinia. There are
major industrial cities such as Milan and
Turin, vineyards, and fields of wheat, corn,
and tomatoes.

The Vatican City, which lies within the
city of Rome, is the smallest independent
state in the world. It is home to the pope,
the head of the Catholic Church.

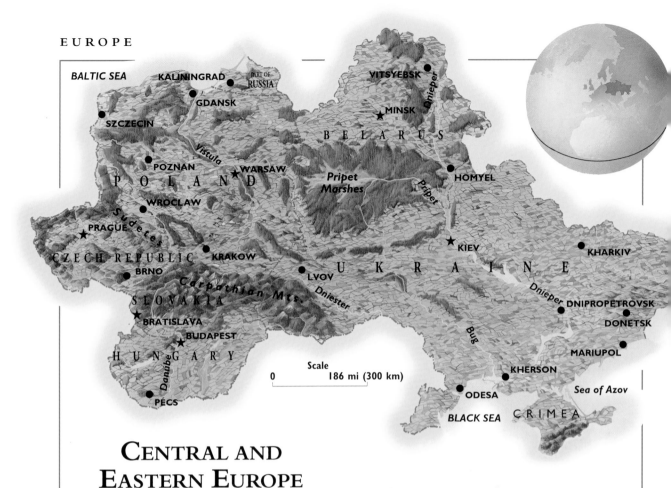

BALTIC SEA
KALININGRAD
PART OF RUSSIA
VITSYEBSK
GDANSK
SZCZECIN
MINSK
BELARUS
Vistula
POZNAN
WARSAW
Pripet Marshes
HOMYEL
POLAND
Pripet
WROCLAW
Sudetes
PRAGUE
KIEV
KHARKIV
CZECH REPUBLIC
KRAKOW
BRNO
LVOV
UKRAINE
Carpathian Mts.
Dniester
Dnieper
DNIPROPETROVSK
SLOVAKIA
DONETSK
BRATISLAVA
Bug
MARIUPOL
BUDAPEST
HUNGARY
KHERSON
Scale
Danube
0   186 mi (300 km)
ODESA
Sea of Azov
PÉCS
BLACK SEA   CRIMEA

CENTRAL AND EASTERN EUROPE

MUCH OF CENTRAL and eastern
Europe is flat, low-lying land. A large part
of this is given over to farming, but native
forest still remains in upland areas, where
elk, wolves, and bison roam. The northern
part of this region has warm summers but
cold winters. Crops such as potatoes and
cereals are grown, and animals are farmed
for their milk and meat.

Heavy industries such as mining, metal-
working, car production, and glass making
are important for the economy of Poland.
Pollution from the burning of coal to
produce electricity, and from factories and
cars, threatens the environment.

In the south, the forested Sudetes and
Carpathian Mountain ranges rim the Czech
Republic and cover much of Slovakia.
Cereals, root vegetables, and livestock are
farmed in the valleys. The fertile lowlands of
Hungary are scattered with orchards and
vineyards. All three countries have vehicle,
chemical, and textile industries.

The undulating lowlands of the Ukraine
with their fertile "black earth" have long

Odesa is a major industrial port on the
south coast of the Ukraine. The warm
waters of the Black Sea have made this
coast a popular destination for tourists.

been intensively cultivated. There are fields
of wheat, barley, sugar beet, and sunflowers.
Manufacturing is concentrated in the
Ukraine's southeastern cities.

The borders of central and eastern
Europe have changed many times over the
years. Until recently, many countries were
controlled by, or were part of, the former
Soviet Union. They are now independent,
and starting to grow in prosperity.

SOUTHEAST EUROPE

THE BALKANS, which make up most of southeast Europe, are lands of rugged mountains and deep valleys. Winters are cold, but cotton, tobacco, and grapes can be grown in the warm summers. Several of these countries were once part of Yugoslavia. The creation of new borders, as well as clashes between ethnic groups, has led to conflict.

Greece is one of the oldest nations in Europe. As a mountainous country, farming space is limited, and its olive groves and vineyards are scattered along the hillsides. Greece has many islands, and a large part of its economy relies on a large shipping industry and tourism.

Slovenian farm buildings have a wooden frame called a *kozolec* to store hay.

The Corinth Canal cuts across a narrow stretch of the Greek mainland to create a sea route.

Turkey is split between Europe and Asia by a narrow stretch of water called the Bosporus. Turkey's coasts are warm, but the dry grasslands of its interior can be bitterly cold in winter. Turkey is famous for its craft industry, especially carpets and pottery. Its Mediterranean coastline and ancient sites also make it a popular tourist destination.

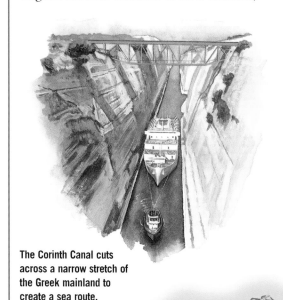

LJUBLJANA
ZAGREB
SLOVENIA
CROATIA
MOLDOVA
CHISINAU
Carpathian Mts
ROMANIA
BOSNIA
BELGRADE
SPLIT
SARAJEVO
Danube
BUCHAREST
YUGOSLAVIA
SOFIA
BULGARIA
BLACK SEA
ADRIATIC SEA
TIRANË
SKOPJE
Bosporus
SAMSUN
MACEDONIA
THESSALONIKI
ISTANBUL
ANKARA
ERZURUM
ALBANIA
Corfu
GREECE
AEGEAN SEA
TURKEY
L. Van
Lesbos
IZMIR
Kefallonia
ATHENS
Khios
L. Tuz
Euphrates
Tigris
ADANA
ANTALYA
Rhodes
Crete
CYPRUS
NICOSIA
Karpathos

Scale
0   186 mi (300 km)

MEDITERRANEAN SEA

RUSSIA

STRETCHING between two continents, Europe and Asia, Russia is the largest country in the world. Until 1991 it was part of the Soviet Union. Most of Russia's population live west of the Ural Mountains, in the European part, many in the big cities of Moscow and St. Petersburg. Also in this area lies a good part of Russia's farmland, producing cereals and root crops.

East of the Ural Mountains is Siberia, a vast area of sparsely populated land. The climate is harsh, with frozen tundra in the north and thick coniferous forest, known as taiga, further south. The deepest lake in the world, Lake Baikal, is found in the southeast. Siberia is rich in coal, oil, gas, and metal ores. The region has a small population, but a large number of different peoples.

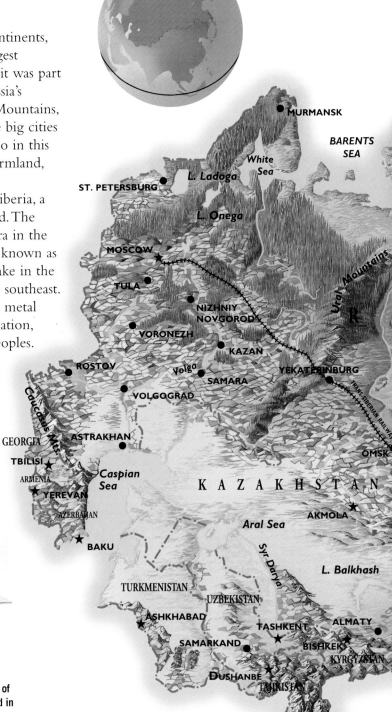

Many old Russian buildings are made of wood. This church stands on an island in Lake Onega, near St. Petersburg.

Scattered around the fringes of the Arctic Ocean are a number of small communities. They herd reindeer or cattle, and use animal skins to keep warm as their ancestors did.

The Trans-Siberian Railway runs from Moscow across the southern part of Siberia. It is a vital link for people and industry between east and west. The longest line in the world, it takes eight days to travel.

Since the collapse of the Soviet Union, Russia, for all its natural mineral wealth, long-established industries and advanced technology, is struggling to develop its economy.

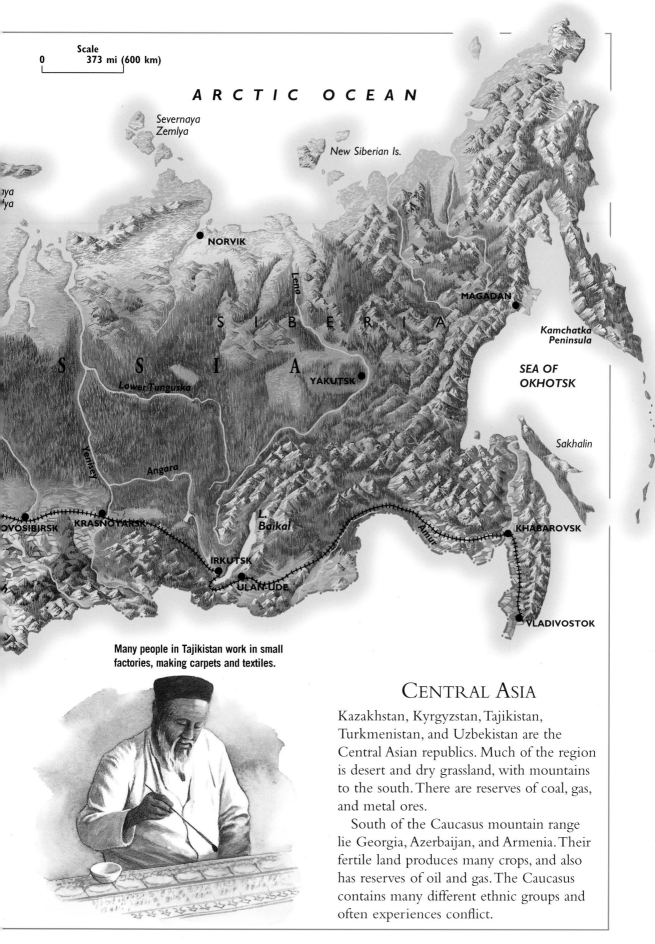

Scale
0   373 mi (600 km)

ARCTIC OCEAN

Severnaya Zemlya

New Siberian Is.

● **NORVIK**

Lena

● **MAGADAN**

Kamchatka Peninsula

S I B E R I A

● **YAKUTSK**

SEA OF OKHOTSK

S S S I A

Lower Tunguska

Sakhalin

Yenisey

Angara

L. *Baikal*

Amur

OVOSIBIRSK ● **KRASNOYARSK**

● **KHABAROVSK**

● **IRKUTSK**

● **ULAN-UDE**

● **VLADIVOSTOK**

Many people in Tajikistan work in small factories, making carpets and textiles.

CENTRAL ASIA

Kazakhstan, Kyrgyzstan, Tajikistan, Turkmenistan, and Uzbekistan are the Central Asian republics. Much of the region is desert and dry grassland, with mountains to the south. There are reserves of coal, gas, and metal ores.

South of the Caucasus mountain range lie Georgia, Azerbaijan, and Armenia. Their fertile land produces many crops, and also has reserves of oil and gas. The Caucasus contains many different ethnic groups and often experiences conflict.

ASIA

ASIA is the largest continent. The northern part is taken up entirely by Russia, where icy tundra and coniferous forests dominate the landscape. Further south are the barren grasslands, or steppes, of Central Asia. These merge into vast areas of desert that are bitterly cold in winter.

Much of southwest Asia, known as the Middle East, is also covered by desert, but this is hot, dry, and often sandy. South of the world's highest mountain range, the Himalayas, the countries of southern Asia have a monsoon climate. Long periods of hot, dry weather are followed by heavy rains. To the southeast, a peninsula reaches out toward the many islands of Indonesia, where important areas of dense tropical rain forest are found.

Large areas of Asia are virtually uninhabited, but Asia still has the largest population of any continent. In the south and east, several countries have become wealthy from their rich reserves of oil or their successful technological industries. In many other countries, however, poverty is rife. Most people farm for a living, and are vulnerable to floods or droughts. Asian cities are growing larger as more and more people move in from the countryside to try to find work.

Kathmandu, the capital of Nepal, lies in a Himalayan valley. Tourists visit Nepal to walk and climb in the mountains with the help of local guides, called sherpas.

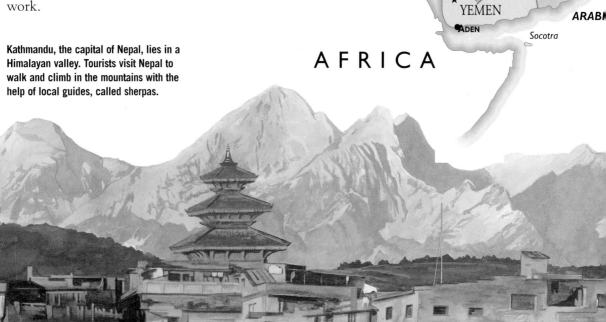

ST. PETERSBURG

MOSCOW ★   NIZI NOV

EUROPE

Volga   SAM

ROSTOV

ISTANBUL   Black Sea   ASTRAKHAN

ANKARA   GEORGIA ·TBILISI

MEDITERRANEAN SEA   TURKEY   ARMENIA   AZERBAIJAN
YEREVAN   BAKU ★   TURK

Caspian Sea

BEIRUT   TABRIZ   ASHKHA
LEBANON ★   SYRIA
ISRAEL   ★ DAMASCUS
JERUSALEM ★ ★ AMMAN   BAGHDAD   ★ TEHRAN
JORDAN

IRAQ   IRAN

BASRA   SHIRAZ
KUWAIT

MEDINA   SAUDI   Persian Gulf
RIYADH ★   BAHRAIN
MAKKAH   QATAR   ABU DHABI
RED SEA   ARABIA   U.A.E.   ★ MU

OMAN

SAN'A ★   ARAB

YEMEN

ADEN   Socotra

AFRICA

Novaya
Zemlya

SIBERIA

U S S I A

Ob
Irtysh

YEKATERINBURG

OMSK ● NOVOSIBIRSK

Yenisey

Lena

YAKUTSK ●

SEA OF OKHOTSK

Sakhalin

Kuril Islands

AKMOLA ★

ZAKHSTAN

L.
Balkhash

ULAN BATOR ★

MONGOLIA

IRKUTSK ●

L.
Baikal

Amur

HARBIN ●

VLADIVOSTOK ●

SHENYANG ●

JAPAN

TOKYO ★
YOKOHAMA ●

Syr Darya

STAN

ASHKENT

ALMATY ●

★BISHKEK
KYRGYZSTAN

ÜRÜMQI ●

BEIJING
● ★
TIANJIN ●

NORTH
KOREA

PYONGYANG ★

★SEOUL

SOUTH
KOREA

KYOTO ●
★
OSAKA ●

KITAKYUSHU ●

SAMARKAND ●

HANBE ★ TAJIKISTAN

KASHI ●

LANZHOU ●

XI'AN ●

Huang

NANJING ●

SHANGHAI ●

Ryukyu Is.

**PACIFIC
OCEAN**

KABUL ●

ANISTAN

Indus

KASHMIR

ISLAMABAD ★

LAHORE ●

IKISTAN

KARACHI ●

DELHI ●
NEW ★
DELHI
KANPUR ●

C H I N A

TIBET

LHASA ●

KATHMANDU ★

N E P A L

BHUTAN

Ganges

DHAKA ★

KOLKATA ●

CHONGQING ●

Yangtse

WUHAN ●

CHANGSHA ●

GUANGZHOU ●

HONG KONG ●

T'AIPEI ★

TAIWAN

AHMADABAD ●

INDIA

BANGLA-
DESH

MANDALAY ●

**BURMA
(MYANMAR)**

HANOI ★

LAOS

Hainan

MANILA ★

PHILIPPINES

MUMBAI ●

HYDERABAD ●

VIANGCHAN ●

**SOUTH CHINA
SEA**

VIETNAM

DAVAO ●

YANGON ★

THAILAND

BANGKOK ★

Mekong

CAMBODIA

BANGALORE ●

CHENNAI ●

BAY OF BENGAL

PNOMH ★
PENH
HO CHI ●
MINH CITY

BRUNEI

*Irian
Jaya*

Andaman Is.

MALAYSIA

Borneo

Sulawesi

COLOMBO ★

SRI LANKA

KUALA LUMPUR
★

ALDIVES

Equator

SINGAPORE

Sumatra

INDONESIA

Timor

INDIAN OCEAN

JAKARTA ●
★ *Java*

SURABAYA ●

Scale

0   621 mi (1000 km)

★   **Capital city**

FACTFILE I

A tiger from South Asia.

SOUTH

Afghanistan   Nepal   Bhutan

Maldives   Sri Lanka   Bangladesh

AFGHANISTAN
Area 251,825 sq miles (652,225 km²) **Pop.**
25,824,882 **Capital** Kabul **Languages** Pashto, Dari

BANGLADESH
Area 55,598 sq miles (143,998 km²) **Pop.**
127,117,967 **Capital** Dhaka **Languages** Bengali,
English

BHUTAN
Area 18,147 sq miles (47,000 km²) **Population**
1,951,965 **Capital** Thimphu **Language** Dzongkha

MALDIVES
Area 115 sq miles (298 km²) **Population** 300,220
Capital Malé **Language** Divehi

NEPAL
Area 56,827 sq miles (147,181 km²) **Pop.**
24,302,653 **Capital** Kathmandu **Language** Nepali

SRI LANKA
Area 24,885 sq miles (64,453 km²) **Pop.**
19,144,895 **Capital** Colombo **Languages**
Sinhalese, Tamil

PAKISTAN

Area 310,404 sq miles (803,943 km²) **Population**
138,123,359 **Capital** Islamabad **Language** Urdu
Religions Muslim 97%, other 3% **Currency**
Pakistan rupee

INDIA

Area 1,269,346 sq miles (3,287,590 km²)
Population 1,000,848,550 **Capital** New Delhi
Languages Hindi, Bengali, Bihari, Telugu,
Marathi, Tamil, English **Religions** Hindu 83%,
Muslim 11%, Christian 2%, Sikh 2%, other 2%
Currency Rupee

WEST AND CENTRAL

Georgia   Azerbaijan

Armenia   Kazakhstan   Turkmenistan

Uzbekistan   Tajikistan   Kyrgyzstan

ARMENIA
Area 11,506 sq miles (29,800 km²) **Population**
3,409,234 **Capital** Yerevan **Language** Armenian

AZERBAIJAN
Area 34,209 sq miles (88,600 km²) **Population**
7,908,224 **Capital** Baku **Language** Azeri

GEORGIA
Area 26,911 sq miles (69,700 km²) **Population**
5,066,499 **Capital** Tbilisi **Language** Georgian

KAZAKHSTAN
Area 1,049,200 sq miles (2,717,300 km²)
Population 16,824,825 **Capital** Akmola
Languages Kazakh, Russian

KYRGYZSTAN
Area 76,641 sq miles (198,500 km²) **Population**
4,546,055 **Capital** Bishkek **Language** Kyrgyz

TAJIKISTAN
Area 55,251 sq miles (143,100 km²) **Pop.**
6,102,854 **Capital** Dushanbe **Language** Tajik

TURKMENISTAN
Area 188,460 sq miles (488,100 km²) **Pop.**
4,366,383 **Capital** Ashkhabad **Language**
Turkmen

UZBEKISTAN
Area 172,740 sq miles (447,400 km²) **Pop.**
24,102,473 **Capital** Tashkent **Language** Uzbek

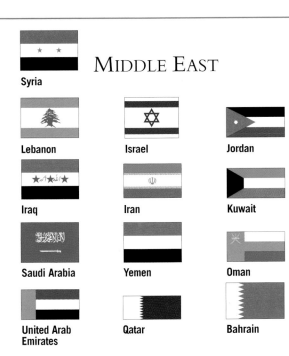

Middle East

Syria

Lebanon   **Israel**   **Jordan**

Iraq   **Iran**   **Kuwait**

Saudi Arabia   **Yemen**   **Oman**

United Arab Emirates   **Qatar**   **Bahrain**

BAHRAIN
Area 266.9 sq miles (691.2 km²) **Population**
629,090 **Capital** Manama **Language** Arabic
Religions Muslim 85%, Christian 7%, other 7%
IRAN
Area 636,300 sq miles (1,648,000 km²)
Population 65,179,752 **Capital** Tehran
Language Farsi **Religions** Muslim 99%,
other 1%
IRAQ
Area 169,235 sq miles (438,317 km²) **Pop.**
22,427,150 **Capital** Baghdad **Language** Arabic
Religions Muslim 97%, other 3%
ISRAEL
Area 8,473 sq miles (21,946 km²) **Population**
5,749,760 **Capital** Jerusalem **Languages** Hebrew,
Arabic **Religions** Jewish 82%, Muslim 14%,
Christian 2%, other 2%
JORDAN
Area 37,738 sq miles (97,740 km²) **Population**
4,561,147 **Capital** Amman **Language** Arabic
Religions Muslim 92%, other 8%
KUWAIT
Area 6,880 sq miles (17,818 km²) **Population**
1,991,115 **Capital** Kuwait **Language** Arabic
Religions Muslim 85%, other 15%
LEBANON
Area 4,036 sq miles (10,452 km²) **Population**
3,562,699 **Capital** Beirut **Language** Arabic
Religions Muslim 75%, Christian 25%

OMAN
Area 105,000 sq miles (271,950 km²) **Population**
2,446,645 **Capital** Muscat **Language** Arabic
Religion Muslim 100%
QATAR
Area 4,416 sq miles (11,437 km²) **Population**
723,542 **Capital** Doha **Language** Arabic
Religions Muslim 95%, other 5%
SAUDI ARABIA
Area 926,933 sq miles (2,400,900 km²)
Population 21,504,613 **Capital** Riyadh
Language Arabic **Religion** Muslim 100%
SYRIA
Area 71,498 sq miles (185,180 km²) **Population**
17,213,891 **Capital** Damascus **Language** Arabic
Religions Muslim 90%, other 10%
UNITED ARAB EMIRATES
Area 29,016 sq miles (75,150 km²) **Population**
2,344,402 **Capital** Abu Dhabi **Language** Arabic
Religions Muslim 96%, other 4%
YEMEN
Area 184,375 sq miles (477,530 km²) **Population**
16,942,230 **Capital** San'a **Language** Arabic
Religions Muslim 97%, other 3%

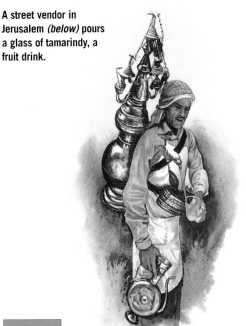

A street vendor in
Jerusalem *(below)* pours
a glass of tamarindy, a
fruit drink.

Turkey

Area 300,948 sq miles (779,452 km²) **Population**
65,599,206 **Capital** Ankara **Language** Turkish
Religions Muslim 99%, other 1% **Currency**
Turkish lira

FACTFILE II

This Hani girl *(above)* is one of the many non-Chinese peoples from Yunnan province in the south of China.

 JAPAN

Area 145,875 sq miles (377,815 km²) **Population** 126,182,077 **Capital** Tokyo **Language** Japanese, **Religions** Shinto and Buddhist 92%, other 8% **Currency** Yen **Highest point** Mount Fuji 12,388 ft (3,776 m) **Main industries** Cars, electronic goods, ships, steel, metals, textiles, telecommunications

 EASTERN

Taiwan

South Korea   North Korea   Mongolia

MONGOLIA
Area 604,250 sq miles (1,565,000 km²) **Population** 2,617,379 **Capital** Ulan Bator **Language** Kalkha Mongol

NORTH KOREA
Area 46,540 sq miles (120,538 km²) **Population** 21,386,109 **Capital** Pyongyang **Language** Korean

SOUTH KOREA
Area 38,310 sq miles (99,222 km²) **Population** 46,884,800 **Capital** Seoul **Language** Korean

TAIWAN
Area 13,741 sq miles (35,590 km²) **Population** 22,113,250 **Capital** Taipei **Language** Chinese

 CHINA

Area 3,695,500 sq miles (9,571,300 km²) **Population** 1,246,871,951 **Capital** Beijing **Language** Chinese (many dialects) **Religions** Confucian, Taoist, Buddhist, Muslim **Currency** Yuan **Highest point** Mount Everest 29,028 ft (8,848 m) **Main industries** Textiles, clothing, iron and steel, fertilizers, weapons, electronics, toys **Major cities** Shanghai (13,659,000), Beijing (11,414,000), Tianjin (10, 687,000), Qingdao (5,124,868), Shenyang (4,655,280)

A traditional funeral procession in South Korea. Most South Koreans are Buddhists or Christians, but some people still hold the ancient belief of shamanism—that a spirit world lies alongside the earthly world. A priest, or shaman (male or female), acts as a link between the worlds.

SOUTHEAST

Philippines

Brunei

Singapore

Burma

Thailand

Malaysia

Cambodia

Laos

Vietnam

A boy from Vietnam.

BRUNEI
Area 2,226 sq miles (5,765 km²) **Population** 322,982 **Capital** Bandar Seri Begawan **Languages** Malay, Chinese **Religions** Muslim 66%, Buddhist 14%, Christian 10%, other 10%

BURMA (MYANMAR)
Area 259,674 sq miles (672,552 km²) **Population** 48,081,302 **Capital** Yangon **Language** Burmese **Religions** Buddhist 89%, Muslim 4%, Christian 4%, other 3%

MALAYSIA
Area 127,320 sq miles (329,758 km²) **Population** 21,376,066 **Capital** Kuala Lumpur **Language** Malay **Religions** Muslim 53%, Buddhist 18%, Chinese religions 11%, Hindu 7%, Christian 7%, other 4%

PHILIPPINES
Area 115,831 sq miles (300,000 km²) **Pop.** 79,345,812 **Capital** Manila **Languages** English, Pilipino **Religions** Roman Catholic 83%, Protestant 9%, Muslim 5%, other 3%

SINGAPORE
Area 238 sq miles (616 km²) **Pop.** 3,531,600 **Languages** Chinese, English, Malay, Tamil **Religions** Taoist 29%, Buddhist 27%, Muslim 16%, Christian 10%, other 18%

THAILAND
Area 198,115 sq miles (513,115 km²) **Pop.** 60,609,046 **Capital** Bangkok **Language** Thai **Religions** Buddhist 95%, other 5%

VIETNAM
Area 126,860 sq miles (328,566 km²) **Population** 76,236,259 **Capital** Hanoi **Languages** Vietnamese, French **Religions** Buddhist 55%, Christian 7%, other 38%

A bridge over the Mekong river in Vietnam.

CAMBODIA
Area 69,898 sq miles (181,035 km²) **Pop.** 11,626,520 **Capital** Phnom Penh **Language** Khmer **Religions** Buddhist 95%, other 5%

LAOS
Area 91,429 sq miles (236,800 km²) **Pop.** 5,407,453 **Capital** Viangchan **Languages** Lao, French **Religions** Buddhist 85%, other 5%

INDONESIA
Area 735,358 sq miles (1,904,569 km²) **Population** 216,108,345 **Capital** Jakarta **Language** Indonesian **Religions** Muslim 87%, Protestant 6%, Catholic 3%, other 4% **Currency** Rupiah

MIDDLE EAST

THE COUNTRIES of southwest Asia are known as the Middle East. Much of this region is covered with mountains or desert, and has a hot, dry climate. The most fertile areas are along the Mediterranean coast and the river floodplains of eastern Iraq. Here, crops such as cereals and citrus fruits can be grown.

Other Middle Eastern countries, such as Saudi Arabia, Kuwait, and the United Arab Emirates, have become very wealthy despite their lack of water and mostly barren land. They have huge reserves of oil, which they export to the rest of the world.

Some Middle Eastern cities date back thousands of years. Many have a pattern of narrow, winding streets around a central market and mosque for worship. Outside Israel, a Jewish state, most people follow the religion of Islam, but there is also frequent conflict between religious and ethnic groups. Border and territorial disputes between countries have also led to wars in the Middle East.

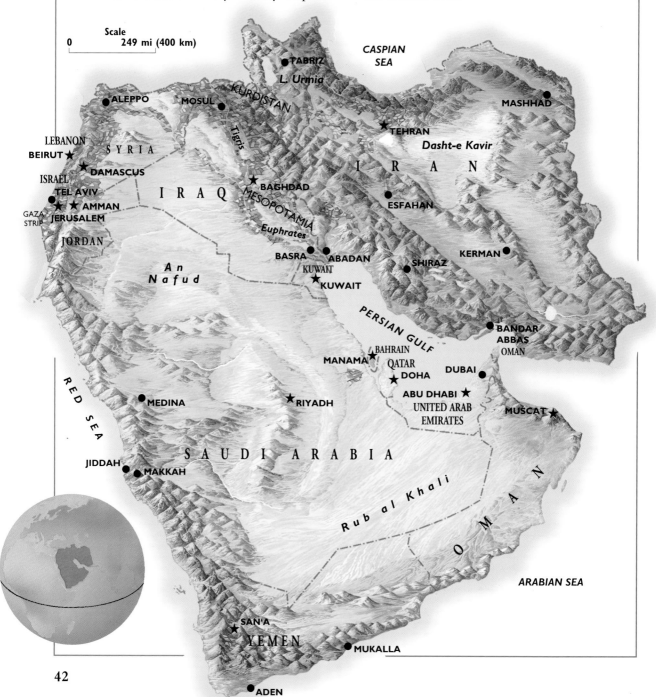

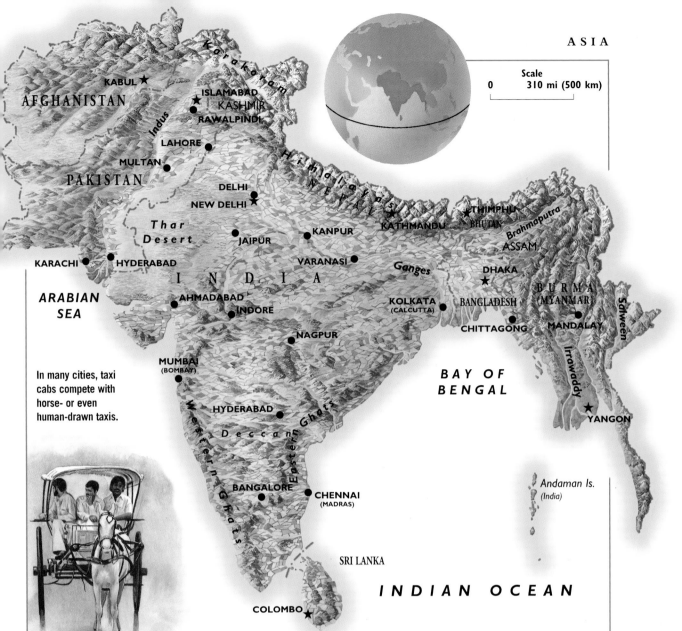

Scale
0   310 mi (500 km)

AFGHANISTAN

KABUL ★

ISLAMABAD ★
KASHMIR
RAWALPINDI

LAHORE ●

MULTAN ●

PAKISTAN

Indus

Karakoram

Himalayas

DELHI ●
NEW DELHI ★

Thar Desert

JAIPUR ●

KANPUR ●

NEPAL

KATHMANDU ★

THIMPHU ★
BHUTAN

Brahmaputra

ASSAM

KARACHI ●

HYDERABAD ●

VARANASI ●

Ganges

DHAKA ●

I N D I A

ARABIAN SEA

AHMADABAD ●

INDORE ●

KOLKATA
(CALCUTTA) ●

BANGLADESH

BURMA
(MYANMAR)

Salween

NAGPUR ●

CHITTAGONG ●

MANDALAY ●

In many cities, taxi cabs compete with horse- or even human-drawn taxis.

MUMBAI
(BOMBAY) ●

BAY OF BENGAL

Irrawaddy

HYDERABAD ●

Deccan

Eastern Ghats

Western Ghats

YANGON ★

BANGALORE ●

CHENNAI
(MADRAS) ●

Andaman Is.
(India)

SRI LANKA

INDIAN OCEAN

COLOMBO ★

SOUTHERN ASIA

THE INDIAN subcontinent encompasses India, Pakistan, Bangladesh, Nepal, Bhutan, and Sri Lanka. Much of the northern region is mountainous, with the Himalaya and Karakoram ranges forming a border with the rest of Asia. A region of desert covers eastern Pakistan and northeast India, bordering areas of more fertile land, where farmers grow rice and cotton. The Ganges Valley is one of the most intensely cultivated regions in the world. Sri Lanka has large tea plantations, and is a popular tourist resort.

Southern Asia is home to many peoples, with thousands of different languages and several religions. But many people are also very poor. Most are farmers who rely on the monsoon rains to water their crops. They suffer badly when there are droughts or floods, especially in low-lying countries such as Bangladesh. Years of civil war have also added to the poverty in Afghanistan and Burma.

However, some Southern Asian countries are becoming more and more industrialized. India has an important manufacturing industry, producing textiles, clothing, and machinery. Its large cities are overcrowded with people who have come from the countryside looking for work.

CHINA

THE THIRD largest country in the world, China also has the highest population—more than one-fifth of all the people in the world today. The west of the country is mountainous, with bleak deserts and grassland plains or steppes. The deserts are freezing cold in winter. The highest point is Mount Everest, which lies on the border between Tibet and Nepal. Tibet used to be an independent country, but has been occupied by China since the 1950s.

In contrast, the eastern part of China has a warm climate, with fertile soil and river valleys. Great rivers, including the Yangtse and the Huang He, or Yellow River, wind their way from the western mountains to the sea. The Grand Canal, the world's longest waterway, stretches for 1,112 miles (1,790 km). Most of the population of China live in the east. China is a major producer of tea, wheat, and sweet potatoes as well as rice, which is grown in the flat, flooded paddies of the south. Pigs and poultry are kept everywhere.

Many Chinese cities have populations of more than a million people. Most people live in apartment blocks. China has natural resources such as coal and oil, and also heavy industry such as steel and chemical plants. It is an important producer of textiles, clothing, and electronics. Though many people in China are poor, it is a rapidly developing country.

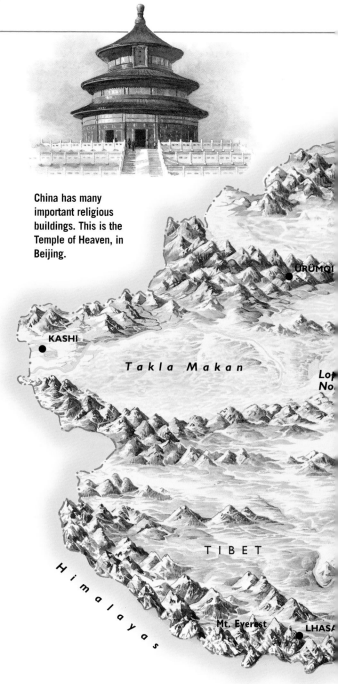

China has many important religious buildings. This is the Temple of Heaven, in Beijing.

URUMQI

KASHI

Takla Makan

Lop Nor

Himalayas

TIBET

Mt. Everest

LHASA

Farmers bring their produce into the city markets to sell.

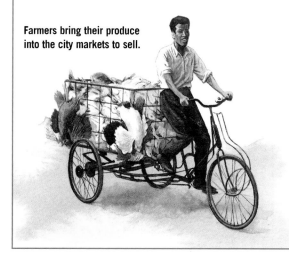

MONGOLIA AND KOREA

Mongolia occupies the grassy plains between the mountains to the north and the Gobi desert to the south. Many people still live a nomadic life on the central plains. Mongolia has coal and oil resources.

North and South Korea are both mountainous and forested, but while North Korea has little contact with the outside world, and relies on enormous state-controlled farms, South Korea has thriving, modern industries and many trade links.

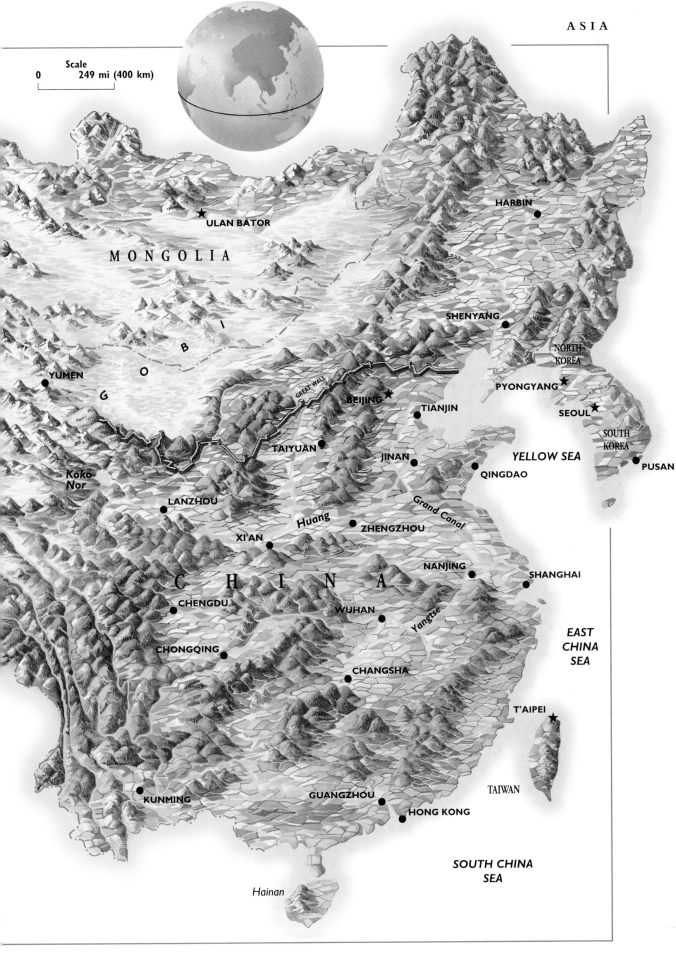

Scale

0   249 mi (400 km)

ULAN BATOR

MONGOLIA

G O B I

YUMEN

Koko
Nor

GREAT WALL

TAIYUAN

LANZHOU

XI'AN

Huang

CHENGDU

CHINA

CHONGQING

KUNMING

HARBIN

SHENYANG

NORTH
KOREA

PYONGYANG

SEOUL

SOUTH
KOREA

PUSAN

BEIJING

TIANJIN

JINAN

QINGDAO

YELLOW SEA

Grand Canal

ZHENGZHOU

NANJING

SHANGHAI

WUHAN

Yangtse

EAST
CHINA
SEA

CHANGSHA

T'AIPEI

TAIWAN

GUANGZHOU

HONG KONG

SOUTH CHINA
SEA

Hainan

SOUTHEAST ASIA

THE SOUTHEAST corner of mainland Asia, together with thousands of islands further south, make up the region of Southeast Asia. On the mainland are the mountainous, forested countries of Thailand, Laos, Vietnam, and Cambodia. Great rivers flow through the region, creating fertile valleys where large quantities of crops such as rice and tropical fruits are grown. Thailand also has successful tourist and manufacturing industries. Cambodia, Vietnam, and Laos have been devastated by war, although Vietnam now has a growing industrial economy.

Malaysia is made up of the mainland Malay peninsula, and most of northern Borneo. Southern Borneo, together with other islands including Sumatra and Java, is part of Indonesia. The climate is hot and wet, with areas of dense rain forest that are home to many kinds of plants and animals. Malaysia and Indonesia are rich in natural resources such as oil, gas, and rubber. They also have strong manufacturing industries.

North of Borneo are the Philippines, thousands of small islands, many of which are uninhabited. Although their country is rich in mineral resources, many people are obliged to leave to find work in other countries. Both the Philippines and Indonesia are frequently threatened by tropical storms, volcanoes, and earthquakes.

The small countries of Singapore and Brunei are among the world's richest countries. While Brunei has huge resources of oil and gas, Singapore is a worldwide center of manufacturing and business.

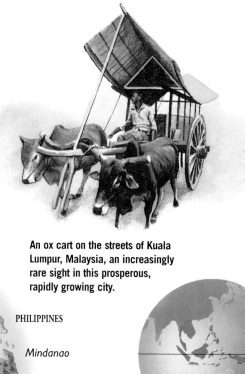

An ox cart on the streets of Kuala Lumpur, Malaysia, an increasingly rare sight in this prosperous, rapidly growing city.

LAOS
★ HANOI
VIANGCHAN
THAILAND
VIETNAM
Mekong
BANGKOK
CAMBODIA
PHNOM PENH ★
● HO CHI MINH CITY
SOUTH CHINA SEA
Luzon
MANILA ★
PHILIPPINES
Mindanao
M A L A Y S I A
● MEDAN
★ KUALA LUMPUR
BRUNEI ★
BANDAR SERI BEGAWAN
SARAWAK
CELEBES SEA
● SINGAPORE
B o r n e o
Sulawesi
Moluccas
PALEMBANG ●
BANJARMASIN
New Guinea
PAPUA NEW GUINEA
PACIFIC OCEAN
I N D O N E S I A
BANDA SEA
JAKARTA ★
J a v a
SURABAYA ●
YOGYAKARTA
Flores
PORT MORESBY ★
Bali
Timor
INDIAN OCEAN

Scale
0   497 mi (800 km)

JAPAN

LYING OFF the east coast of mainland Asia, Japan is made up of four large islands, where most of the population live, and thousands of smaller ones. The four main islands are Honshu, Hokkaido, Kyushu, and Shikoku. Much of Japan is covered with mountains, some of them volcanic. It is also densely forested. Winter is cold in the north, but the south of the country has mild winters and hot summers.

With limited land available for farming, and a lack of natural resources, Japan has turned to industry and technology for its livelihood. Today, it is a leading producer of cars, ships, and electronic goods such as computers, televisions, and cameras. It is also a powerful financial center. Most people live in the cities, several of which have a population of over one million. Their buildings are designed to withstand the earthquakes that frequently occur.

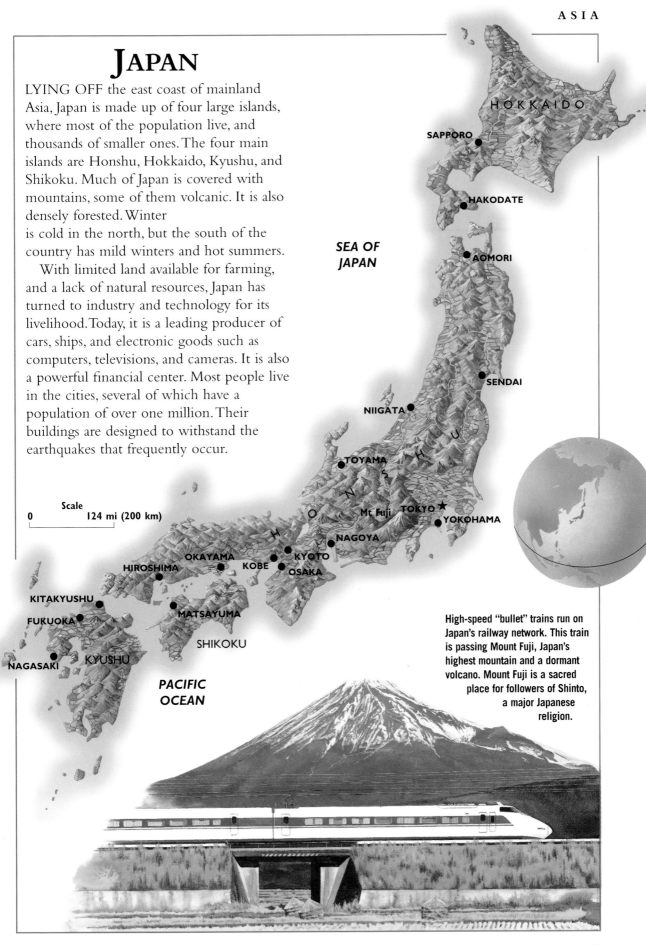

HOKKAIDO

SAPPORO

HAKODATE

SEA OF JAPAN

AOMORI

SENDAI

NIIGATA

H O N S H U

TOYAMA

Mt Fuji   TOKYO ★
NAGOYA   YOKOHAMA

KYOTO
OKAYAMA   KOBE
HIROSHIMA   OSAKA

KITAKYUSHU

FUKUOKA   MATSAYUMA

SHIKOKU

NAGASAKI   KYUSHU

PACIFIC OCEAN

Scale
0 ——— 124 mi (200 km)

High-speed "bullet" trains run on Japan's railway network. This train is passing Mount Fuji, Japan's highest mountain and a dormant volcano. Mount Fuji is a sacred place for followers of Shinto, a major Japanese religion.

OCEANIA

STRETCHING ACROSS a vast region of the Pacific Ocean, Oceania is made up of the large island of Australia (almost a continent in itself) together with New Zealand, Papua New Guinea, and thousands of small Pacific islands.

Much of Australia is covered with hot, dry desert and flat, open grassland known as the outback. Most people live in towns and cities near the coasts, especially the south coast. Papua New Guinea, in contrast, is a country of high mountains and dense rain forests. Many tribes of native peoples live in mountain valleys so isolated that they have only recently come into contact with the outside world.

New Zealand is made up of two islands, the north of which is warm and volcanic, while the south island is cooler, with mountains and forests. The grassy lowlands are fertile, and ideal for farming. The remote position of New Zealand, and also of Australia and Papua New Guinea, means that they are home to animals that are not found anywhere else in the world.

The world's longest coral reef, the Great Barrier Reef, stretches for 1,243 miles (2,000 km) along the northeastern coast of Australia.

The Pacific islands are the remains of volcanoes that have erupted beneath the ocean. Some islands, such as Hawaii, still have active volcanoes. The islands are grouped together into nations. Some of these are independent, while others, such as New Caledonia, are colonies of European countries or the United States. Many Pacific islands are very beautiful, with rich vegetation and a warm climate. This makes them popular tourist destinations, and also gives them plenty of fertile land for farming crops.

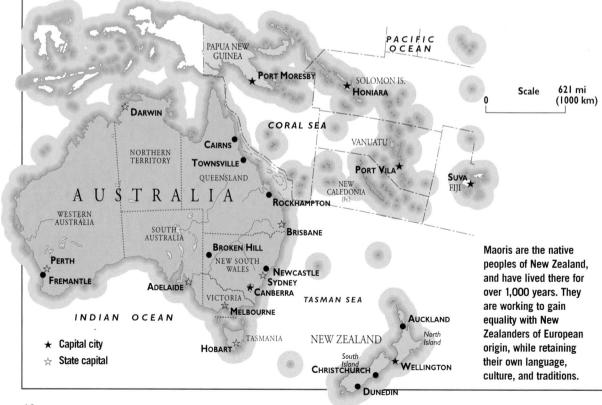

PACIFIC OCEAN

PAPUA NEW GUINEA

★ PORT MORESBY

★ SOLOMON IS.
★ HONIARA

Scale 621 mi
0 (1000 km)

DARWIN

CORAL SEA

VANUATU

NORTHERN TERRITORY

CAIRNS

TOWNSVILLE

QUEENSLAND

PORT VILA ★

NEW CALEDONIA (Fr.)

SUVA ★
FIJI

A U S T R A L I A

WESTERN AUSTRALIA

ROCKHAMPTON

☆ BRISBANE

SOUTH AUSTRALIA

BROKEN HILL

NEW SOUTH WALES

PERTH

NEWCASTLE

☆ FREMANTLE

ADELAIDE ☆

SYDNEY
★ CANBERRA

VICTORIA

TASMAN SEA

☆ MELBOURNE

INDIAN OCEAN

AUCKLAND

North Island

★ Capital city
☆ State capital

TASMANIA

NEW ZEALAND

South Island

HOBART

CHRISTCHURCH ★ WELLINGTON

DUNEDIN

Maoris are the native peoples of New Zealand, and have lived there for over 1,000 years. They are working to gain equality with New Zealanders of European origin, while retaining their own language, culture, and traditions.

FACTFILE

Stilt house, Solomon Islands.

PACIFIC ISLANDS

Papua New Guinea

Nauru

Kiribati

Solomon Islands

Tuvalu

Fiji

Vanuatu

Samoa

Tonga

AUSTRALIA

Area 2,966,153 sq miles (7,682,300 km²)
Population 18,783,551 **Capital** Canberra
Language English **Religions** Anglican 26%,
Roman Catholic 26%, other Christian 24%, other
24% **Currency** Australian dollar **Highest point**
Mount Kosciusko 7,310 ft (2,228 m)

NEW ZEALAND

Area 104,454 sq miles (270,534 km²) **Pop.**
3,662,265 **Capital** Wellington **Languages**
English, Maori **Religions** Protestant 47%, Roman
Catholic 15%, other 22%, nonreligious 16%
Currency New Zealand dollar

A Maori girl.

FIJI
Area 7,095 sq miles (18,376 km²) **Pop.** 812,918
Capital Suva **Languages** Fijian, Hindi, English
KIRIBATI
Area 313 sq miles (811 km²) **Pop.** 85,501 **Capital**
Tarawa **Languages** I-Kiribati, English
NAURU
Area 8 sq miles (21 km²) **Pop.** 10,605 **Capital**
Yaren District **Languages** Nauruan, English
PAPUA NEW GUINEA
Area 178,704 sq miles (462,840 km²) **Pop.**
4,705,126 **Capital** Port Moresby **Languages**
Pidgin, English, Motu

A duck-billed platypus.

SAMOA
Area 1,093 sq miles (2831 km²) **Population**
229,979 **Capital** Apia **Languages** Samoan, English
SOLOMON ISLANDS
Area 10,639 sq miles (27,556 km²) **Pop.** 455,429
Capital Honiara **Languages** English, Pidgin
TONGA
Area 289 sq miles (748 km²) **Pop.** 109,082
Capital Nuku'alofa **Languages** Tongan, English
TUVALU
Area 10 sq miles (26 km²) **Pop.** 10,588 **Capital**
Funafuti **Languages** Tuvaluan, English
VANUATU
Area 4,707 sq miles (12,190 km²) **Population**
189,036 **Capital** Port Vila **Languages** Bislama,
English, French

AUSTRALIA

APART FROM a long range of mountains running down its eastern side, most of Australia is flat, hot, and dry. It is rich in natural resources such as coal and minerals including gold, copper, and iron. The vast interior, or outback, is mostly desert, or dry scrublands. To the east, this gives way to

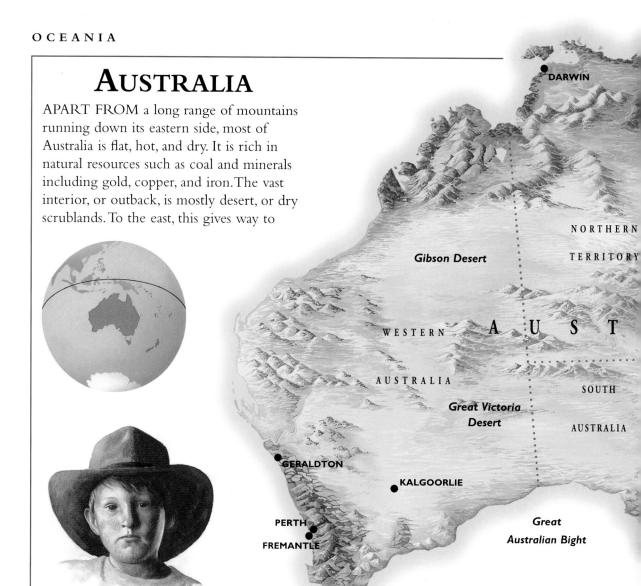

Gibson Desert

NORTHERN
TERRITORY

WESTERN

A U S T

AUSTRALIA

SOUTH

Great Victoria
Desert

AUSTRALIA

DARWIN

GERALDTON

KALGOORLIE

Great
Australian Bight

PERTH
FREMANTLE

An Australian boy. On the most isolated cattle and sheep stations, far from towns, children must learn their lessons at home. If there is a medical emergency, doctors fly in by airplane.

open grassland—stock-raising country, where Australia's sheep and cattle ranches, or "stations," are situated. With its millions of sheep, Australia is the world's largest producer of wool.

Most Australians live around the coasts, where the climate is cooler and the land fertile. Crops such as wheat and tropical fruits are grown for export, and vineyards produce world-famous wines. A high proportion of people live in the largest cities, such as Sydney, Brisbane, and Melbourne. The cities have modern manufacturing industries.

Sydney Harbor Bridge, and the famous Opera House.

Scale
0   310 mi (500 km)

Cape
York
Peninsula

CAIRNS

Great Barrier Reef

Great Dividing Range

QUEENSLAND

ROCKHAMPTON

L I A

Eyre

BRISBANE

Darling

NEW SOUTH
WALES

BROKEN
HILL

NEWCASTLE

Murray

SYDNEY

ADELAIDE

CANBERRA

VICTORIA

MELBOURNE

TASMAN
SEA

TASMANIA

HOBART

New Zealand is home to
several kinds of birds that
have lost the ability to fly
because of a lack of
natural predators. One of
these, the kiwi, has
become the symbol of
New Zealand. Others
include the rare takahe
(left), which lives in the
mountains of South Island.

NEW ZEALAND

Like its neighbor, Australia, New Zealand is
a prosperous country. It farms huge
numbers of cattle and sheep, producing
large quantities of wool, meat, and dairy
products for export. Its fertile land and
warm climate also make it ideal for
vineyards and fruit and vegetables. The
power of New Zealand's many rivers, and
also the underground heat from volcanic
activity on North Island, are harnessed
through nonpolluting electricity schemes.

The native peoples of New Zealand are
the Maoris, who originally came from
Polynesia. They still make up about nine
percent of the population, and have retained
much of their culture and traditions.

AUCKLAND

NORTH
ISLAND

NEW ZEALAND

SOUTH
ISLAND

Southern Alps

WELLINGTON

CHRISTCHURCH

DUNEDIN

Stewart I.

About 200 years ago, the British and
other Europeans began to arrive on the
shores of Australia. They routed many of the
native Australians already living there, and
seized their land. Today, much of Australia's
population is of European descent, although
there are substantial numbers of immigrants
from Asia. The small number of native
Australians that remain are working to
reclaim some of their land and sacred sites.

New Zealand includes two main
islands, North Island and South
Island, and several smaller ones.
Most people live on North Island.

AFRICA

THE SECOND largest continent after Asia, Africa is almost completely surrounded by water, apart from the narrow point at which it joins Asia. The north of the continent is mostly hot, barren desert, edged with coastal areas that are cooler and wetter in winter.

Further south, the desert gives way to areas of flat grassland. The equator runs right through the center of Africa. The countries on or close to the equator are dominated by the largest area of tropical rain forest outside South America. Here the climate is hot and wet.

Scale
0 ————— 621 mi (1000 km)

★ Capital city

This member of the Bamilike people of Cameroon in central Africa wears a feathered hat and elephant mask for a special ceremony.

Wodaabe girl from Niger.

The rain forest is home to many different plants and animals, including gorillas and chimpanzees. Many rivers weave their way through central Africa. To the east and south are large areas of open grassland scattered with trees, known as savanna. Animals such as elephants, zebra, and wildebeest roam the savanna, along with predators such as lions, wild dogs, and hyenas.

AFRICAN PEOPLES

North of the Sahara desert, the people of Africa are mainly Arabs and Berbers, who follow the religion of Islam. South of the Sahara, most people are black. They follow a variety of religions. Much of Africa was at one time controlled by Europe, and today people of European descent still live there, mostly in the south.

Africa exports its natural resources of metals and oil, as well as crops such as coffee and cocoa. However, many African countries are poor compared to the rest of the world. Few have established manufacturing industries. Most people live in the countryside, and rely on producing only enough crops, or farming enough cattle to support their families. They suffer from frequent droughts, floods, and periods of starvation. Wars between and within countries also threaten their lives.

SAHARA DESERT

THE WORLD'S largest desert, the Sahara stretches across an area of Northern Africa that is almost the size of the United States. It is constantly growing larger as the sparse grassland at its edges dies away. The Sahara is a hot desert, where rain may fail to fall for years on end. During the day, temperatures can reach over 122°F (50°C) in the shade, but nights are often cold. There are areas of sand that often drift into large dunes, but much of the Sahara is made up of rocky ground and mountains.

Despite these harsh conditions, the Sahara desert is not without life. Animals that are specially adapted for life with little water and intense heat can survive there. Many take shelter in burrows during the day, coming out at night to feed.

People also live in the Sahara desert. Small towns are able to survive around oases in the desert. Groups of nomads also travel across the harsh landscape to trade in the town markets. For thousands of years, they carried their goods and supplies by camel, an animal that can cope extremely well with desert life. It also provided the nomads with milk and meat. Today motor vehicles are more often used to cross the desert.

An oasis is a place in the desert where water comes up from beneath the ground. Here the land is fertile, and crops such as dates and olives can be grown. Towns are built around oases, forming stopping-off points on desert roads.

FACTFILE I

A Berber girl from Morocco.

NORTHEAST

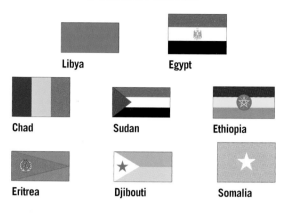

Libya   Egypt

Chad   Sudan   Ethiopia

Eritrea   Djibouti   Somalia

NORTHWEST

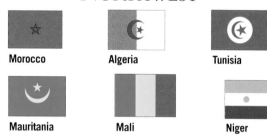

Morocco   Algeria   Tunisia

Mauritania   Mali   Niger

ALGERIA
Area 919,600 sq miles (2,381,741 km²) **Pop.** 31,133,486 **Capital** Algiers **Languages** Arabic, French

MALI
Area 478,841 sq miles (1,240,192 km²) **Pop.** 10,429,124 **Capital** Bamako **Language** French

MAURITANIA
Area 397,956 sq miles (1,030,700 km²) **Population** 2,581,738 **Capital** Nouakchott **Languages** Arabic, Poular, Wolof, Solinke

MOROCCO
Area 172,414 sq miles (446,550 km²) **Population** 29,661,636 **Capital** Rabat **Languages** Arabic, Berber, Spanish, French

NIGER
Area 489,191 sq miles (1,267,000 km²) **Population** 9,962,242 **Capital** Niamey **Languages** French, Hausa, Tuareg, Djerma, Fulani

TUNISIA
Area 63,379 sq miles (164,150 km²) **Population** 9,513,603 **Capital** Tunis **Languages** Arabic, Berber, French

CHAD
Area 495,755 sq miles (1,284,000 km²) **Population** 7,557,436 **Capital** N'Djamena **Languages** French, Arabic

DJIBOUTI
Area 8,958 sq miles (23,200 km²) **Pop.** 447,439 **Capital** Djibouti **Languages** Arabic, French

EGYPT
Area 385,229 sq miles (997,739 km²) **Pop.** 67,273,906 **Capital** Cairo **Language** Arabic

ERITREA
Area 46,774 sq miles (121,144 km²) **Pop.** 3,984,723 **Capital** Asmera **Language** Tigrinya

ETHIOPIA
Area 435,609 sq miles (1,128,221 km²) **Pop.** 59,680,383 **Capital** Addis Ababa **Language** Amharic

LIBYA
Area 685,524 sq miles (1,775,500 km²) **Pop.** 4,992,838 **Capital** Tripoli **Language** Arabic

SOMALIA
Area 246,201 sq miles (637,657 km²) **Population** 7,140,643 **Capital** Mogadishu **Languages** Somali, Arabic, English, Italian

SUDAN
Area 967,500 sq miles (2,505,813 km²) **Population** 34,475,690 **Capital** Khartoum **Languages** Arabic, English

 # NIGERIA

Area 356,669 sq miles (923,768 km²) **Population** 113,828,587 **Capital** Abuja **Languages** English, Hausa, Yoruba, Ibo **Religions** Muslim 50%, Christian 40%, Animist 10% **Currency** Naira

WEST

Senegal	Gambia	Cape Verde
Guinea-Bissau	Guinea	Sierra Leone
Liberia	Côte d'Ivoire	Burkina Faso
Ghana	Togo	Benin
Cameroon	Central African Republic	São Tomé and Príncipe

BENIN
Area 43,484 sq miles (112,622 km²) **Population** 6,305,567 **Capital** Porto-Novo **Language** French

BURKINA FASO
Area 105,869 sq miles (274,200 km²) **Population** 11,575,898 **Capital** Ouagadougou **Languages** French, Mossi

CAMEROON
Area 183,569 sq miles (475,442 km²) **Population** 15,456,090 **Capital** Yaoundé **Languages** French, English

CAPE VERDE ISLANDS
Area 1,557 sq miles (4033 km²) **Population** 405,748 **Capital** Praia **Languages** Portuguese, Crioulo

CENTRAL AFRICAN REPUBLIC
Area 240,536 sq miles (622,984 km²) **Population** 3,444,950 **Capital** Bangui **Languages** French, Sango

CÔTE D'IVOIRE
Area 124,503 sq miles (322,462 km²) **Population** 15,818,068 **Capitals** Yamoussoukro, Abidjan **Languages** French, Malinke

GAMBIA
Area 4,361 sq miles (11,295 km²) **Population** 1,336,320 **Capital** Banjul **Language** English

GHANA
Area 92,100 sq miles (238,537 km²) **Population** 18,887,626 **Capital** Accra **Languages** English, Kwa languages

GUINEA
Area 94,926 sq miles (245,857 km²) **Population** 7,538,953 **Capital** Conakry **Languages** French, Soussou, Manika

GUINEA-BISSAU
Area 13,948 sq miles (36,125 km²) **Population** 1,234,555 **Capital** Bissau **Language** Portuguese

LIBERIA
Area 37,743 sq miles (97,754 km²) **Population** 2,923,725 **Capital** Monrovia **Language** English

SÃO TOMÉ AND PRÍNCIPE
Area 372 sq miles (964 km²) **Population** 154,878 **Capital** São Tomé **Language** Portuguese

SENEGAL
Area 75,750 sq miles (196,192 km²) **Pop.** 10,051,930 **Capital** Dakar **Language** French

SIERRA LEONE
Area 27,699 sq miles (71,740 km²) **Population** 5,296,651 **Capital** Freetown **Languages** English, Krio, Mende, Limba, Temne

TOGO
Area 21,925 sq miles (56,785 km²) **Population** 5,081,423 **Capital** Lomé **Languages** French, Kabiye

An African market.

FACTFILE II

Maasai girl from Kenya. The Maasai are nomadic cattle herders.

EAST

Kenya

Uganda

Tanzania

Rwanda

Burundi

Malawi

Mozambique

Seychelles

Comoros

CENTRAL

Congo

Angola

Zambia

Equatorial Guinea

Gabon

Congo-Brazzaville

ANGOLA
Area 481,354 sq miles (1,246,700 km²)
Population 11,177,537 **Capital** Luanda
Languages Portuguese, Bantu languages
CONGO
Area 905,365 sq miles (2,344,885 km²)
Population 50,481,305 **Capital** Kinshasa
Languages Swahili, Lingala, French
CONGO-BRAZZAVILLE
Area 132,047 sq miles (342,000 km²) **Pop.**
2,716,814 **Capital** Brazzaville **Language** French
EQUATORIAL GUINEA
Area 10,831 sq miles (28,051 km²) **Pop.** 465,746
Capital Malabo **Language** Spanish
GABON
Area 103,347 sq miles (267,667 km²) **Pop.**
1,225,853 **Capital** Libreville **Languages** French,
Fang, Bantu languages
ZAMBIA
Area 290,586 sq miles (752,614 km²) **Pop.**
9,663,535 **Capital** Lusaka **Languages** English, Lozi

BURUNDI
Area 10,747 sq miles (27,834 km²) **Population**
5,735,937 **Capital** Bujumbura **Languages**
French, Kirundi, Swahili
COMOROS
Area 719 sq miles (1862 km²) **Population**
562,723 **Capital** Moroni **Languages** Arabic,
French
KENYA
Area 224,081 sq miles (580,367 km²) **Population**
28,808,658 **Capital** Nairobi **Languages** Swahili,
English, Kikuyu, Luo
MALAWI
Area 45,747 sq miles (118,484 km²) **Population**
10,000,416 **Capital** Lilongwe **Languages**
English, Chichewa
MOZAMBIQUE
Area 308,642 sq miles (799,380 km²) **Population**
19,124,335 **Capital** Maputo **Languages**
Portuguese, Ronga, Shangaan, Muchope
RWANDA
Area 10,169 sq miles (26,338 km²) **Population**
8,154,933 **Capital** Kigali **Languages** French,
Kinyarwanda, Swahili
SEYCHELLES
Area 175 sq miles (454 km²) **Population**
76,164 **Capital** Victoria **Languages** English,
Creole
TANZANIA
Area 364,900 sq miles (945,087 km²) **Population**
31,270,820 **Capital** Dodoma **Languages** Swahili,
English
UGANDA
Area 93,104 sq miles (241,139 km²) **Population**
22,804,973 **Capital** Kampala **Languages** English,
Luganda

SOUTHERN

Namibia

Botswana

South Africa

Lesotho

Swaziland

Madagascar

Mauritius

Zimbabwe

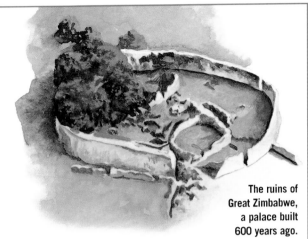
The ruins of Great Zimbabwe, a palace built 600 years ago.

BOTSWANA
Area 224,712 sq miles (582,000 km²) **Population** 1,464,167 **Capital** Gaborone **Languages** English, Tswana

LESOTHO
Area 11,720 sq miles (30,355 km²) **Population** 2,128,950 **Capital** Maseru **Languages** English, Sesotho

MADAGASCAR
Area 226,658 sq miles (587,041 km²) **Population** 14,873,387 **Capital** Antananarivo **Languages** Malagasy, French

MAURITIUS
Area 788 sq miles (2040 km²) **Pop.** 1,182,212 **Capital** Port Louis **Languages** English, Creole

NAMIBIA
Area 318,261 sq miles (824,292 km²) **Population** 1,648,270 **Capital** Windhoek **Languages** English, Afrikaans, German

SOUTH AFRICA
Area 471,445 sq miles (1,221,037 km²) **Pop.** 43,426,386 **Capitals** Pretoria, Cape Town **Languages** Afrikaans, English, Xhosa, Zulu, Sesotho

SWAZILAND
Area 6,704 sq miles (17,363 km²) **Pop.** 985,335 **Capital** Mbabane **Languages** English, siSwati

ZIMBABWE
Area 150,873 sq miles (390,759 km²) **Population** 11,163,160 **Capital** Harare **Languages** English, Shona, Ndebele

A flat-topped mountain called Table Mountain overlooks the city of Cape Town, in South Africa. The city lies near the Cape of Good Hope.

NORTHERN AFRICA

THE NORTHERN half of Africa stretches down from the fertile coast bordering the Mediterranean Sea, through vast areas of desert and savanna, into the forests of the west and central Africa. Apart from the Atlas Mountains, the Ethiopian Highlands and Saharan ranges, much of the region is a level plateau.

In the far north of Africa, the countries bordering the coast benefit from natural resources of oil and gas. They also rely on tourism and the manufacture of textiles and carpets. The population are mostly Arabs. Berbers, an ancient native people, live in the uplands of Morocco.

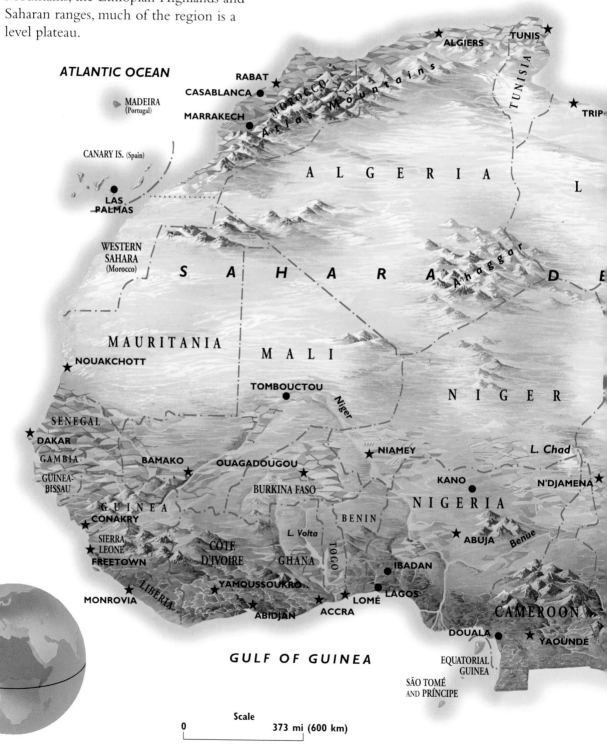

ATLANTIC OCEAN

ALGIERS

TUNIS

TUNISIA

RABAT

MOROCCO

CASABLANCA

Atlas Mountains

MADEIRA
(Portugal)

MARRAKECH

TRIP

CANARY IS. (Spain)

ALGERIA

L

LAS
PALMAS

WESTERN
SAHARA
(Morocco)

S A H A R A

Ahaggar

D

MAURITANIA

MALI

NOUAKCHOTT

N I G E R

TOMBOUCTOU

Niger

SENEGAL

DAKAR

NIAMEY

L. Chad

GAMBIA

BAMAKO

OUAGADOUGOU

KANO

N'DJAMENA

GUINEA-
BISSAU

BURKINA FASO

N I G E R I A

G U I N E A

BENIN

CONAKRY

ABUJA

Benue

SIERRA
LEONE

L. Volta

FREETOWN

CÔTE
D'IVOIRE

GHANA

TOGO

IBADAN

LAGOS

MONROVIA

YAMOUSSOUKRO

LOMÉ

LIBERIA

ABIDJAN

ACCRA

CAMEROON

DOUALA

YAOUNDÉ

GULF OF GUINEA

EQUATORIAL
GUINEA

SÃO TOMÉ
AND PRÍNCIPE

Scale

0   373 mi (600 km)

South of the Sahara, agriculture is the primary industry of many countries. Rivers such as the Nile, Niger and Senegal provide essential water with which to irrigate crops. However, in many countries such as Mauritania and Mali, drought is a recurrent problem. In the driest areas, nomadic cattle-herders travel vast distances in search of good grazing.

There are many different peoples living in northern Africa. Conflict between them often leads to long and devastating wars. The combination of war, drought and widespread poverty has led to terrible famines in Ethiopia and Sudan.

West Africa has a wetter climate, and crops such as coffee, bananas, cocoa, peanuts, and citrus fruits are grown. For many years, timber has been an important product of countries such as the Côte d'Ivoire (Ivory Coast), but this was carried out at such a rate that vast areas of the forest have now disappeared. Mining of oil and metal ores is a rich resource, but due to poor government and frequent wars, many countries are still impoverished.

Many people in northern Africa live in small towns or villages, producing just enough food and goods for themselves. Others crowd into the cities, looking for work. They often have to live in very poor conditions on the outskirts of the city.

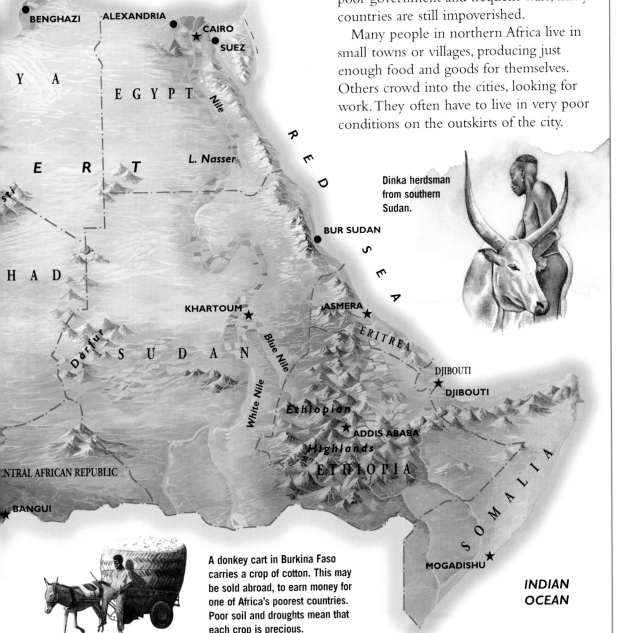

MEDITERRANEAN SEA

BENGHAZI
ALEXANDRIA
CAIRO
SUEZ
Y A
E G Y P T
Nile
L. Nasser
E R T
R E D
H A D
BUR SUDAN
S E A
Dinka herdsman from southern Sudan.
KHARTOUM
ASMERA
ERITREA
S U D A N
Darfur
Blue Nile
DJIBOUTI
DJIBOUTI
White Nile
Ethiopian
ADDIS ABABA
Highlands
ETHIOPIA
NTRAL AFRICAN REPUBLIC
S O M A L I A
BANGUI
MOGADISHU
INDIAN OCEAN

A donkey cart in Burkina Faso carries a crop of cotton. This may be sold abroad, to earn money for one of Africa's poorest countries. Poor soil and droughts mean that each crop is precious.

SOUTHERN AFRICA

THE CONGO basin covers much of central Africa. Here, the mighty Congo River winds through dense rain forest, where animals such as the rare mountain gorilla, and a host of bird species live.

To the south and east are high plateaux, with a cooler, drier climate. Much of the land is flat grassland, called savanna, where animals such as giraffes, elephants, and lions roam. In the southwest, the savanna gives way to areas of hot, dry desert. In the east,

deep valleys, high volcanic mountains and huge lakes have formed along a split in the earth's crust, known as the Great Rift Valley.

Southern Africa is rich in natural resources such as oil, metals (particularly copper and gold), and diamonds. Mining is therefore a vitally important industry. Tourism is also important to the savanna regions, where large national parks have been set up to protect the wildlife. In the eastern highlands, crops of tea and coffee are grown for export. Cattle are farmed for their meat and dairy products.

This Mozambique woman wears cream made from ground bark on her skin to protect it from the sun. Mozambique was ruled by Portugal until it became independent in 1975.

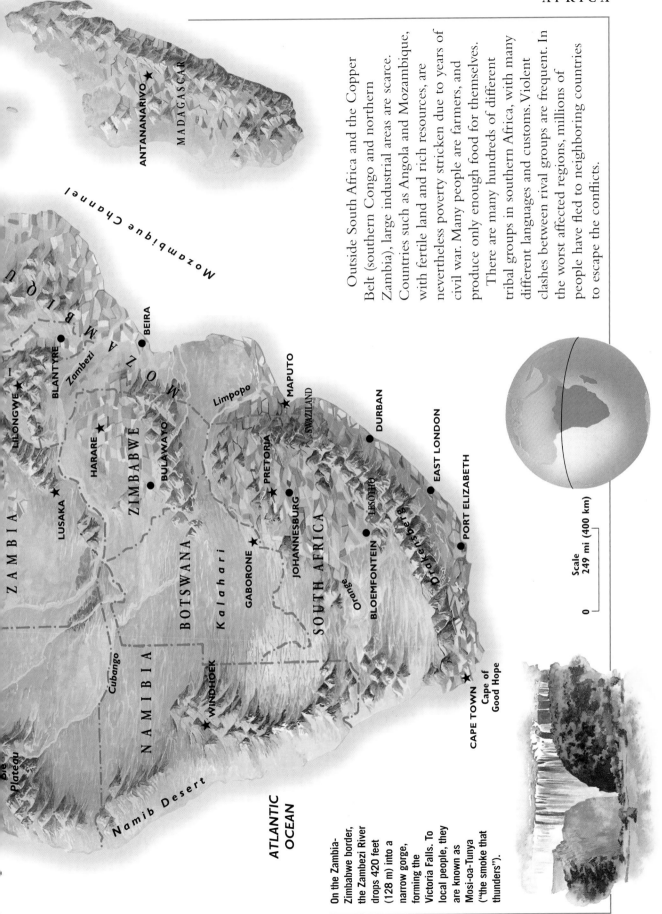

Outside South Africa and the Copper Belt (southern Congo and northern Zambia), large industrial areas are scarce. Countries such as Angola and Mozambique, with fertile land and rich resources, are nevertheless poverty stricken due to years of civil war. Many people are farmers, and produce only enough food for themselves.

There are many hundreds of different tribal groups in southern Africa, with many different languages and customs. Violent clashes between rival groups are frequent. In the worst affected regions, millions of people have fled to neighboring countries to escape the conflicts.

On the Zambia-Zimbabwe border, the Zambezi River drops 420 feet (128 m) into a narrow gorge, forming the Victoria Falls. To local people, they are known as Mosi-oa-Tunya ("the smoke that thunders").

Scale
0   249 mi (400 km)

ANTANANARIVO
MADAGASCAR

Mozambique Channel

BEIRA
Zambezi
BLANTYRE
LILONGWE
Limpopo
MAPUTO
SWAZILAND
DURBAN
HARARE
ZIMBABWE
BULAWAYO
PRETORIA
EAST LONDON
LUSAKA
JOHANNESBURG
LESOTHO
PORT ELIZABETH
ZAMBIA
BOTSWANA
Kalahari
GABORONE
BLOEMFONTEIN
Drakensberg
Orange
SOUTH AFRICA
Cubango
NAMIBIA
WINDHOEK
ATLANTIC OCEAN
CAPE TOWN
Cape of Good Hope
Namib Desert
Plateau